# THE ITINERARY OF
# BENJAMIN OF TUDELA

Copyright © 2008 BiblioBazaar
All rights reserved

Original copyright: 1907

# THE ITINERARY OF BENJAMIN OF TUDELA

Critical Text, Translation and
Commentary by
Marcus Nathan Adler

# THE ITINERARY OF
BENJAMIN OF TUDELA

DEDICATED TO THE MEMORY OF

MORITZ STEINSCHNEIDER

# CONTENTS

INTRODUCTION ................................................................................. 11

I. ISLAM IN THE MIDDLE AGES. ..................................................... 11

II. THE OBJECT OF BENJAMIN'S JOURNEY. ............................... 17

III. BIBLIOGRAPHY. ............................................................................ 19

HEBREW INTRODUCTION. .............................................................. 23

# INTRODUCTION

## I.

## ISLAM IN THE MIDDLE AGES.

The Itinerary of Benjamin of Tudela throws a flashlight upon one of the most interesting stages in the development of nations.

The history of the civilized world from the downfall of the Roman Empire to the present day may be summarized as the struggle between Cross and Crescent. This struggle is characterized by a persistent ebb and flow. Mohammed in 622 A.D. transformed, as if by magic, a cluster of Bedouin tribes into a warlike people. An Arabian Empire was formed, which reached from the Ebro to the Indus. Its further advance was stemmed in the year 732, just a hundred years after Mohammed's death, by Charles Martel, in the seven days' battle of Tours.

The progress of the culture of the Arabs was as rapid as had been that of their arms. Great cities such as Cairo and Bagdad were built. Commerce and manufactures flourished. The Jews, who enjoyed protection under the benign rule of the Caliphs, transmitted to the Arabs the learning and science of the Greeks. Schools and universities arose in all parts of the Empire. The dark age of Christendom proved to be the golden age of literature for Jew and Arab.

By the eleventh century, however, the Arabs had lost much of their martial spirit. Islam might have lost its ascendancy in the East had not the warlike Seljuk Turks, coming from the highlands of Central Asia, possessed themselves of the countries which, in days of old, constituted the Persian Empire under Darius. The Seljuks became ready converts to Islam, and upheld the failing strength of the Arabs.

It was the ill-treatment by the Seljuks of the Christian pilgrims to Palestine which aroused Christian Europe and led to the First Crusade. The feudal system adopted by the Seljuks caused endless dissension among their petty sovereigns, called "Atabegs", all of whom were nominally vassals of the Caliph at Bagdad. Thus it came about that Islamism, divided against itself, offered but a poor resistance to the advance of the Christians. The Crusaders had little difficulty in making their way to Palestine. They captured Jerusalem, and established the Latin kingdom there.

By the middle of the twelfth century Mohammedan power had shrunk to smaller dimensions. Not only did the Franks hold Palestine and all the important posts on the Syrian coast, but, by the capture of Lesser Armenia, Antioch, and Edessa, they had driven a wedge into Syria, and extended their conquests even beyond the Euphrates.

At length there came a pause in the decline of Islam. Zengi, a powerful Seljuk Atabeg, in 1144 captured Edessa, the outpost of Christendom, and the Second Crusade, led by the Emperor Conrad of Germany and by King Louis VII of France, failed to effect the recapture of the fortress. Nureddin, the far-sighted son and successor of Zengi, and later on Saladin, a Kurd, trained at his court, discovered how to restore the fallen might of Islam and expel the Franks from Asia. A necessary preliminary step was to put an end to the dissensions of the Atabeg rulers. Nureddin did this effectually by himself annexing their dominions. His next step was to gain possession of Egypt, and thereby isolate the Latin Kingdom. Genoa, Pisa, and Venice, the three Italian republics who between them had command of the sea, were too selfish and too intent upon their commercial interests to interfere with the designs of the Saracens. The Latin king Amalric had for some years sought to gain a foothold in Egypt. In November, 1168, he led the Christian army as far as the Nile, and was about to seize Fostat, the old unfortified Arab metropolis of Egypt. The inhabitants, however, preferred to set fire to the city rather than that it should fall into the hands of the Christians. To this very day many traces may be seen in the neighbourhood of Cairo of this conflagration. Nureddin's army, in which Saladin held a subordinate command, by a timely arrival on the scene forced the Franks to retreat, and the Saracens were acclaimed as deliverers.

The nominal ruler of Egypt at that time was El-Adid, the Fatimite Caliph, and he made Saladin his Vizier, little thinking that that modest officer would soon supplant him. So efficiently did Saladin administer the country that in a few months it had regained its prosperity, despite the five years' devastating war which had preceded.

At this juncture the traveller Rabbi Benjamin came to Egypt. Some three years earlier he had left his native place—Tudela, on the Ebro in the north of Spain. After passing through the prosperous towns which lie on the Gulf of Lyons, he visited Rome and South Italy. From Otranto he crossed over to Corfu, traversed Greece, and then came to Constantinople, of which he gives an interesting account. Very telling, for example, are the words: "They hire from amongst all nations warriors called Barbarians to fight with the Sultan of the Seljuks; for the natives are not warlike, but are as women who have no strength to fight." After visiting the Islands of the Aegean, as well as Rhodes and Cyprus, he passed on to Antioch, and followed the well-known southern route skirting the Mediterranean, visiting the important cities along the coast, all of which were then in the hands of the Franks.

Having regard to the strained relations between the Christians and Saracens, and to the fights and forays of the Latin knights, we can understand that Benjamin had to follow a very circuitous way to enable him to visit all the places of note in Palestine. From Damascus, which was then the capital of Nureddin's empire, he travelled along with safety until he reached Bagdad, the city of the Caliph, of whom he has much to tell.

It is unlikely that he went far into Persia, which at that time was in a chaotic state, and where the Jews were much oppressed. From Basra, at the mouth of the Tigris, he probably visited the island of Kish in the Persian Gulf, which in the Middle Ages was a great emporium of commerce, and thence proceeded to Egypt by way of Aden and Assuan.

Benjamin gives us a vivid sketch of the Egypt of his day. Peace and plenty seemed to prevail in the country. This happy state of things was entirely due to the wise measures taken by Saladin, who, however, kept himself so studiously in the background, that not even his name is mentioned in the Itinerary. The deposition of the Fatimite Caliph on Friday, September 10, 1171, and his subsequent death, caused little stir. Saladin continued to govern Egypt as Nureddin's lieutenant. In due course he made himself master of Barca and Tripoli; then he conquered Arabia Felix and the Soudan, and after Nureddin's death he had no difficulty in annexing his old master's dominions. The Christian nations viewed his rapidly growing power with natural alarm.

About that time news had reached Europe that a powerful Christian king named Prester John, who reigned over a people coming from Central Asia, had invaded Western Asia and inflicted a crushing defeat upon a Moslem army. Pope Alexander III conceived the hope that a useful ally could be found in this priest-king, who would support and uphold the Christian dominion in Asia. He accordingly dispatched his physician Philip on a mission to this mysterious potentate to secure his help against the Mohammedans. The envoy never returned.

Benjamin is one of the very few writers of the Middle Ages who gives us an account of these subjects of Prester John. They were no other than the infidels, the sons of Ghuz, or Kofar-al-Turak, the wild flat-nosed Mongol hordes from the Tartary Steppes, who, in Benjamin's quaint language, "worship the wind and live in the wilderness, who eat no bread and drink no wine, but feed on uncooked meat. They have no noses—in lieu thereof they have two small holes through which they breathe."

These were not men likely to help the Christians. On the contrary, as is so fully described in Benjamin's Itinerary, they broke the power of Sultan Sinjar, the mighty Shah of Persia, who, had he been spared by the men of Ghuz, would have proved a serious menace to Saladin.

It took Saladin some years to consolidate his empire.

In 1187 he felt himself in a position to engage the Franks in a decisive conflict. At the battle of Tiberias, Guy, the Latin king, was defeated and taken prisoner. The Knights-Templars and Hospitalers, of whose doings at Jerusalem Benjamin gives us particulars, either shared the fate of the king or were slain in action. Jerusalem fell soon afterwards. Pope Alexander III roused the conscience of Europe, and induced the pick of chivalry to embark upon the Third Crusade in 1189. But the prowess of the Emperor Frederic Barbarossa, the gallantry of Richard I of England, the astuteness of Philip Augustus of France, were of no avail. The Fourth and Fifth Crusades were equally unsuccessful, and the tide of Islam's success rose high.

After Saladin's death his empire gradually crumbled to pieces, and under Ghenghis Khan an invasion took place of hordes of Mongols and Tartars, of whom the Ghuz had been merely the precursors. They overran China and Russia, Persia, and parts of Western Asia. The effete Caliphate at Bagdad was overthrown, but to Islam itself fresh life was imparted. The rapid decline of the Mongol power at the end of the thirteenth century gave free scope to the rise of the Ottoman Turks, who had been driven from their haunts east of the Caspian Sea. Like their kinsmen the Seljuks they settled in Asia Minor, and embraced the Mohammedan faith, an example which many Mongols followed. The converts proved trusty warriors to fight the cause of Islam, which gradually attained the zenith of success. On May 29, 1453, Constantinople was captured by the Turks, and an end was made of the Byzantine Empire. Eastern Europe was subsequently overrun by them, and it was not until John Sobieski defeated the Turks under the walls of Vienna in 1683 that their victorious career was checked.

Then at last the tide of Islam turned, and its fortunes have been ebbing ever since. At the present day little territory remains to them in Europe. India and Egypt are now subject to England; Russia has annexed Central Asia; France rules Algiers and Tunis. One wonders whether there will be a pause in this steady decline of Islam, and whether the prophetic words of Scripture will continue to hold good: "He will be a wild man, his hand will be against every man, and every man's hand against him, and he shall dwell in the presence of all his brethren."

This brief consideration of the struggle between Cross and Crescent may serve to indicate the importance of the revival of Islam, which took place between the Second and Third Crusades, at the time when Benjamin wrote his Itinerary.

## II.

## THE OBJECT OF BENJAMIN'S JOURNEY.

We may ask what induced Benjamin to undertake his travels? What object or mission was he carrying out?

It must be explained that the Jew in the Middle Ages was much given to travel. He was the Wandering Jew, who kept up communications between one country and another. He had a natural aptitude for trade and travel. His people were scattered to the four corners of the earth. As we can see from Benjamin's Itinerary, there was scarcely a city of importance where Jews could not be found. In the sacred tongue they possessed a common language, and wherever they went they could rely upon a hospitable reception from their co-religionists. Travelling was, therefore, to them comparatively easy, and the bond of common interest always supplied a motive. Like Joseph, the traveller would be dispatched with the injunction: "I pray thee see whether it be well with thy brethren, and bring me word again."

If this was the case in times when toleration and protection were extended to the Jews, how much stronger must have grown the desire for intercommunication at the time of the Crusades. The most prosperous communities in Germany and the Jewish congregations that lay along the route to Palestine had been exterminated or dispersed, and even in Spain, where the Jews had enjoyed complete security for centuries, they were being pitilessly persecuted in the Moorish kingdom of Cordova.

It is not unlikely, therefore, that Benjamin may have undertaken his journey with the object of finding out where his expatriated brethren might find an asylum. It will be noted that Benjamin seems to use every effort to trace and to afford particulars of independent communities of Jews, who had chiefs of their own, and owed no allegiance to the foreigner.

He may have had trade and mercantile operations in view. He certainly dwells on matters of commercial interest with considerable detail. Probably he was actuated by both motives, coupled with the pious wish of making a pilgrimage to the land of his fathers.

Whatever his intentions may have been, we owe Benjamin no small debt of gratitude for handing to posterity records that form a unique contribution to our knowledge of geography and ethnology in the Middle Ages.

# III.

# BIBLIOGRAPHY.

"The Itinerary of Rabbi Benjamin of Tudela," prepared and published by A. Asher, is the best edition of the diary of that traveller. The first volume appeared in 1840, and contained a carefully compiled Hebrew text with vowel points, together with an English translation and a bibliographical account. A second volume appeared in 1841 containing elaborate notes by Asher himself and by such eminent scholars as Zunz and Rapoport, together with a valuable essay by the former on the Geographical Literature of the Jews and on the Geography of Palestine, also an Essay by Lebrecht on the Caliphate of Bagdad.

In addition to twenty-three several reprints and translations enumerated by Asher, various others have since appeared from time to time, but all of them are based upon the two editions of the text from which he compiled his work. These were the Editio Princeps, printed by Eliezer ben Gershon at Constantinople, 1543, and the Ferrara Edition of 1556, printed by Abraham Usque, the editor of the famous "Jews" Bible in Spanish.

Asher himself more than once deplores the fact that he had not a single MS. to resort to when confronted by doubtful or divergent readings in the texts before him.

I have, however, been fortunate enough to be able to trace and examine three complete MSS. of Benjamin's Travels, as well as large fragments belonging to two other MSS., and these I have embodied in my present collation. The following is a brief description of the MSS.:—

1. BM, a MS. in the British Museum (No. 27,089). It is bound up with some of Maimonides' works, several Midrashic tracts, a commentary on the Hagadah by Joseph Gikatilia, and an extract from Abarbanel's commentary on Isaiah; it forms part of the Almanzi collection, which curiously enough was purchased by the British Museum from Asher & Co. in October, 1865, some twenty years after Asher's death.

Photographs of three pages of this MS. will be found with the Hebrew text. With regard to the date of the MS., some competent judges who have seen it assign it to the thirteenth century, and this view has some support from Professor S. D. Luzzatto, who, in Steinschneider's *Hammazkir* (vol. V, fo. 105, xvii) makes the following comment upon it:—

מסעות ר' בנימין י"ג דפים כתיבה אטבנטית קדומה יותר:

This MS. is the groundwork of the text I have adopted.

2. R, or the Roman MS., in the Casanatense library at Rome, and numbered No. 216 in the Catalogue Sacerdote. This MS. occupies the first twenty-seven leaves of Codex 3097, which contains fifteen other treatises, among them a text of Eldad Hadani, all written by the same scribe, Isaac of Pisa, in 5189 A.M., which corresponds with 1429-1430 (see Colophon at the end of the Hebrew text, page עע). Under my direction Dr. Grünhut, of Jerusalem, proceeded to Rome, and made a copy. Subsequently I obtained a collation of it made by the late Dr. Neubauer; both have been used in preparing the notes to the text. Later on, after the Hebrew text had already been printed, I visited Rome, and on examining the MS. I found that a few variants had been overlooked. I had facsimiles made of several pages, which will be found with the Hebrew text.

3. E, a MS. now in the possession of Herr Epstein of Vienna, who acquired it from Halberstamm's collection. The only reliable clue as to the date of this MS. is the license of the censor: "visto per me fra Luigi da Bologna Juglio 1599." Herr Epstein considers it to have been written at the end of the fifteenth or beginning of the sixteenth century. The MS. is on paper and in "Italian" handwriting. It contains seventy-four quarto pages of from 19-20 lines each. Speaking generally it is analogous to the edition of Ferrara, 1556, which was used by Ashor as the groundwork of his text (Asher, p. 3), but the spelling of persons and places in E often differs from that in the text of Asher.

4. O, in the Oppenheim collection of the Bodleian Library (MS. Opp. add. 8° 36; ff. 58-63; Neubauer 2425), is a fragment. Its first three leaves are continuous, beginning at p. 61 of Asher's edition and ending at p. 73. After this there is a *lacuna* of four leaves, and the fragment, which recommences at p. 98 of Asher's edition, is then continuous to the end of the book. The volume in which it is bound contains various other treatises written by the same scribe, and includes a fragment on Maimonides, whose death is mentioned as occurring in 1202, and also part of a controversy of Nachmanides which took place in 1263.

The MS. is in Spanish Rabbinic characters, and would appear to have been written in the fourteenth or fifteenth century. For the collation of this and the following fragment I am indebted to the kindness of my friend Mr. A. Cowley, of Oxford. Photographs of pages of both MSS. will be found with the Hebrew text.

5. B, also in the Oppenheim collection of the Bodleian Library (MS. Opp. add. 8°, 58; fol. 57; Neubauer 2580). This fragment begins at p. 50 of Asher's edition. The date of this fragment is probably much later than that of O, and may well be as late as the eighteenth century. It appears to be written in an oriental hand.

In addition to the critical text, I give a translation of the British Museum MS., and add brief notes thereto. I have purposely confined the latter to small dimensions in view of the fact that Asher's notes, the Jewish

Encyclopaedia, and the works of such writers as Graetz and others, will enable the reader to acquire further information on the various incidents, personages, and places referred to by Benjamin. I would, however, especially mention a work by Mr. C. Raymond Beazley entitled "The Dawn of Modern Geography," particularly his second volume, published in 1901. The frank and friendly manner in which the writer does justice to the merits of the Jewish traveller contrasts favourably with the petty and malignant comments of certain non-Jewish commentators, of which Asher repeatedly complains.

It is not out of place to mention that soon after the publication in 1841 of the work on Benjamin by A. Asher, there appeared a review thereof in consecutive numbers of the Jewish periodical *Der Orient*. The articles bore the signature *Sider*, but the author proved to be Dr. Steinschneider. They were among the first literary contributions by which he became known. Although written sixty-five years ago his review has a freshness and a value which renders it well worth reading at the present day. The ninetieth birthday of the Nestor of Semitic literature was celebrated on March 30 of last year, and it afforded no little gratification to the writer that Dr. Steinschneider on that occasion accepted the dedication to him of this the latest contribution to the "Benjamin Literature." The savant passed away on the 23rd of January last, and I humbly dedicate my modest work to his memory.

I have the pleasure of expressing my thanks to the editors of the *Jewish Quarterly Review*, who have permitted me to reprint my articles; also to Dr. Berlin and other friends for their co-operation; and to the Delegates of the Oxford University Press for allowing me to make use of the map of Western Asia in the twelfth century, which was designed by Professor S. Lane-Poole.

Marcus N. Adler. *May 27, 1907.*

\* \* \* \* \*

# HEBREW INTRODUCTION.

THIS is the book of travels, which was compiled by Rabbi Benjamin, the son of Jonah, of the land of Navarre—his repose be in Paradise.

The said Rabbi Benjamin set forth from Tudela, his native city, and passed through many remote countries, as is related in his book. In every place which he entered, he made a record of all that he saw, or was told of by trustworthy persons—matters not previously heard of in the land of Sepharad[1]. Also he mentions some of the sages and illustrious men residing in each place. He brought this book with him on his return to the country of Castile, in the year 4933 (C.E. 1173)[2]. The said Rabbi Benjamin is a wise and understanding man, learned in the Law and the Halacha, and wherever we have tested his statements we have found them accurate, true to fact and consistent; for he is a trustworthy man.

His book commences as follows:—I journeyed first from my native town to the city of Saragossa[3], and thence by way of the River Ebro to Tortosa. From there I went a journey of two days to the ancient city of Tarragona with its Cyclopean and Greek buildings[4]. The like thereof is not found among any of the buildings in the country of Sepharad. It is situated by the sea, and two days' journey from the city of Barcelona, where there is a holy congregation, including sages, wise and illustrious men, such as R. Shesheth[5], R. Shealtiel, R. Solomon, and R. Abraham, son of Chisdai. This is a small city and beautiful, lying upon the sea-coast. Merchants come thither from all quarters with their wares, from Greece, from Pisa, Genoa, Sicily, Alexandria in Egypt, Palestine, Africa and all its coasts. Thence it is a day and a half to Gerona, in which there is a small congregation of Jews[6]. A three days'journey takes one to Narbonne, which is a city pre-eminent for learning; thence the Torah (Law) goes forth to all countries. Sages, and great and illustrious men abide here. At their head is R. Kalonymos, the son of the great and illustrious R. Todros of the seed of David, whose pedigree is established. He possesses hereditaments and lands given him by the ruler of the city, of which no man can forcibly dispossess him[7]. Prominent in the community is R Abraham[8], head of the Academy: also R. Machir and R. Judah, and many other distinguished scholars. At the present day 300 Jews are there.

Thence it is four parasangs[9] to the city of Beziers, where there is a congregation of learned men. At their head is R. Solomon Chalafta, R Joseph, and R. Nethanel. Thence it is two days to Har Gaash which is called Montpellier. This is a place well situated for commerce. It is about a parasang from the sea, and men come for business there from all quarters, from Edom, Ishmael, the land of Algarve[10], Lombardy, the dominion of Rome the Great, from all the land of Egypt, Palestine, Greece, France, Asia and England. People of all nations are found there doing business through the medium of the Genoese and Pisans. In the city there are scholars of great eminence, at their head being R. Reuben, son of Todros, R. Nathan, son of Zechariah, and R. Samuel, their chief rabbi, also R. Solomon and R. Mordecai. They have among them houses of learning devoted to the study of the Talmud. Among the community are men both rich and charitable, who lend a helping hand to all that come to them.

From Montpellier it is four parasangs to Lunel, in which there is a congregation of Israelites, who study the Law day and night. Here lived Rabbenu Meshullam the great rabbi, since deceased, and his five sons, who are wise, great and wealthy, namely: R. Joseph, R. Isaac, R. Jacob, R. Aaron, and R. Asher, the recluse, who dwells apart from the world; he pores over his books day and night, fasts periodically and abstains from all meat[11]. He is a great scholar of the Talmud. At Lunel live also their brother-in-law R. Moses, the chief rabbi, R. Samuel the elder[12], R. Ulsarnu, R. Solomon Hacohen, and R. Judah the Physician, the son of

Tibbon, the Sephardi. The students that come from distant lands to learn the Law are taught, boarded, lodged and clothed by the congregation, so long as they attend the house of study. The community has wise, understanding and saintly men of great benevolence, who lend a helping hand to all their brethren both far and near. The congregation consists of about 300 Jews—may the Lord preserve them.

From there it is two parasangs to Posquières, which is a large place containing about forty Jews, with an Academy under the auspices of the great Rabbi, R. Abraham, son of David, of blessed memory, an energetic and wise man, great as a talmudical authority[13]. People come to him from a distance to learn the Law at his lips, and they find rest in his house, and he teaches them. Of those who are without means he also pays the expenses, for he is very rich. The munificent R. Joseph, son of Menachem, also dwells here, and R. Benveniste, R. Benjamin, R. Abraham and R. Isaac, son of R. Meir of blessed memory. Thence it is four parasangs to the suburb (Ghetto?) Bourg de St. Gilles, in which place there are about a hundred Jews. Wise men abide there; at their head being R. Isaac, son of Jacob, R. Abraham, son of Judah, R. Eleazar, R. Jacob, R. Isaac, R. Moses and R. Jacob, son of rabbi Levi of blessed memory. This is a place of pilgrimage of the Gentiles who come hither from the ends of the earth. It is only three miles from the sea, and is situated upon the great River Rhone, which flows through the whole land of Provence. Here dwells the illustrious R. Abba Mari, son of the late R. Isaac; he is the bailiff of Count Raymond[14].

Thence it is three parasangs to the city of Arles, which has about 200 Israelites, at their head being R. Moses, R. Tobias, R. Isaiah, R. Solomon, the chief rabbi R. Nathan, and R. Abba Mari, since deceased[15].

From there it is two days' journey to Marseilles[16], which is a city of princely and wise citizens, possessing two congregations with about 300 Jews. One congregation dwells below on the shore by the sea, the other is in the castle above. They form a great academy of learned men, amongst them being R. Simeon, R. Solomon, R. Isaac, son of Abba

Mari[17], R. Simeon, son of Antoli, and R. Jacob his brother; also R. Libero. These persons are at the head of the upper academy. At the head of the congregation below are R. Jacob Purpis[18], a wealthy man, and R. Abraham, son of R. Meir, his son-in-law, and R. Isaac, son of the late R. Meir. It is a very busy city upon the sea-coast.

From Marseilles one can take ship and in four days reach Genoa, which is also upon the sea. Here live two Jews, R. Samuel, son of Salim, and his brother, from the city of Ceuta, both of them good men. The city is surrounded by a wall, and the inhabitants are not governed by any king, but by judges whom they appoint at their pleasure. Each householder has a tower to his house, and at times of strife they fight from the tops of the towers with each other. They have command of the sea. They build ships which they call galleys, and make predatory attacks upon Edom and Ishmael[19] and the land of Greece as far as Sicily, and they bring back to Genoa spoils from all these places. They are constantly at war with the men of Pisa. Between them and the Pisans there is a distance of two days' journey.

Pisa is a very great city, with about 10,000 turreted houses for battle at times of strife. All its inhabitants are mighty men. They possess neither king nor prince to govern them, but only the judges appointed by themselves. In this city are about twenty Jews, at their head being R. Moses, R. Chayim, and R. Joseph. The city is not surrounded by a wall. It is about six miles from the sea; the river which flows through the city provides it with ingress and egress for ships.

From Pisa it is four parasangs to the city of Lucca, which is the beginning of the frontier of Lombardy. In the city of Lucca are about forty Jews. It is a large place, and at the head of the Jews are R. David, R. Samuel, and R. Jacob.

Thence it is six days' journey to the great city of Rome. Rome is the head of the kingdoms of Christendom, and contains about 200 Jews, who occupy an honourable position and pay no tribute, and amongst them are officials of the Pope Alexander, the spiritual head of all Christendom.

Great scholars reside here, at the head of them being R. Daniel, the chief rabbi, and R. Jechiel, an official of the Pope[20]. He is a handsome young man of intelligence and wisdom, and he has the entry of the Pope's palace; for he is the steward of his house and of all that he has. He is a grandson of R. Nathan, who composed the Aruch[21] and its commentaries. Other scholars are R. Joab, son of the chief rabbi R. Solomon, R. Menachem, head of the academy, R. Jechiel, who lives in Trastevere, and R. Benjamin, son of R. Shabbethai of blessed memory. Rome is divided into two parts by the River Tiber. In the one part is the great church which they call St. Peter's of Rome. The great Palace of Julius Caesar was also in Rome[22].

There are many wonderful structures in the city, different from any others in the world. Including both its inhabited and ruined parts, Rome is about twenty-four miles in circumference. In the midst thereof[23] there are eighty palaces belonging to eighty kings who lived there, each called Imperator, commencing from King Tarquinius down to Nero and Tiberius, who lived at the time of Jesus the Nazarene, ending with Pepin, who freed the land of Sepharad from Islam, and was father of Charlemagne.

There is a palace outside Rome (said to be of Titus). The Consul and his 300 Senators treated him with disfavour, because he failed to take Jerusalem till after three years, though they had bidden him to capture it within two[24].

In Rome is also the palace of Vespasianus, a great and very strong building; also the Colosseum[25], in which edifice there are 365 sections, according to the days of the solar year; and the circumference of these palaces is three miles. There were battles fought here in olden times, and in the palace more than 100,000 men were slain, and there their bones remain piled up to the present day. The king caused to be engraved a representation of the battle and of the forces on either side facing one another, both warriors and horses, all in marble, to exhibit to the world the war of the days of old.

In Rome there is a cave which runs underground, and catacombs of King Tarmal Galsin and his royal consort who are to be found there, seated upon their thrones, and with them about a hundred royal personages. They are all embalmed and preserved to this day. In the church of St. John in the Lateran there are two bronze columns taken from the Temple, the handiwork of King Solomon, each column being engraved "Solomon the son of David." The Jews of Rome told me that every year upon the 9th of Ab they found the columns exuding moisture like water. There also is the cave where Titus the son of Vespasianus stored the Temple vessels which he brought from Jerusalem. There is also a cave in a hill on one bank of the River Tiber where are the graves of the ten martyrs[26]. In front of St. John in the Lateran there are statues of Samson in marble, with a spear in his hand, and of Absalom the son of King David, and another of Constantinus the Great, who built Constantinople and after whom it was called. The last-named statue is of bronze, the horse being overlaid with gold[27]. Many other edifices are there, and remarkable sights beyond enumeration.

From Rome it is four days to Capua, the large town which King Capys built. It is a fine city, but its water is bad, and the country is fever-stricken[28]. About 300 Jews live there, among them great scholars and esteemed persons, at their heads being R. Conso, his brother R. Israel, R. Zaken and the chief rabbi R. David, since deceased. They call this district the Principality.

From there one goes to Pozzuoli which is called Sorrento the Great, built by Zur, son of Hadadezer, when he fled in fear of David the king. The sea has risen and covered the city from its two sides, and at the present day one can still see the markets and towers which stood in the midst of the city[29]. A spring issues forth from beneath the ground containing the oil which is called petroleum. People collect it from the surface of the water and use it medicinally. There are also hot-water springs to the number of about twenty, which issue from the ground and are situated near the sea, and every man who has any disease can go and bathe in them and get cured. All the afflicted of Lombardy visit it in the summertime for that purpose.

From this place a man can travel fifteen miles along a road under the mountains, a work executed by King Romulus who built the city of Rome. He was prompted to this by fear of King David and Joab his general[30]. He built fortifications both upon the mountains and below the mountains reaching as far as the city of Naples. Naples is a very strong city, lying upon the sea-board, and was founded by the Greeks. About 500 Jews live here, amongst them R. Hezekiah, R. Shallum, R. Elijah Hacohen and R. Isaac of Har Napus, the chief rabbi of blessed memory.

Thence one proceeds by sea to the city of Salerno, where the Christians have a school of medicine. About 600 Jews dwell there. Among the scholars are R. Judah, son of R. Isaac, the son of Melchizedek, the great Rabbi[31], who came from the city of Siponto; also R. Solomon (the Cohen), R. Elijah the Greek, R. Abraham Narboni, and R. Hamon. It is a city with walls upon the land side, the other side bordering on the sea and there is a very strong castle on the summit of the hill. Thence it is half a day's journey to Amalfi, where there are about twenty Jews, amongst them R. Hananel, the physician, R. Elisha, and Abu-al-gir, the prince. The inhabitants of the place are merchants engaged in trade, who do not sow or reap, because they dwell upon high hills and lofty crags, but buy everything for money. Nevertheless, they have an abundance of fruit, for it is a land of vineyards and olives, of gardens and plantations, and no one can go to war with them.

Thence it is a day's journey to Benevento, which is a city situated between the sea-coast and a mountain, and possessing a community of about 200 Jews. At their head are R. Kalonymus, R. Zarach, and R. Abraham. From there it is two days' journey to Melfi in the country of Apulia, which is the land of Pul[32], where about 200 Jews reside, at their head being R. Achimaaz, R. Nathan, and R. Isaac. From Melfi it is about a day's journey to Ascoli, where there are about forty Jews, at their head being R. Consoli, R. Zemach, his son-in-law, and R. Joseph. From there it takes two days to Trani on the sea, where all the pilgrims gather to go to Jerusalem; for the port is a convenient one. A community of about 200 Israelites is there, at their head being R. Elijah, R. Nathan, the expounder, and R. Jacob. It is a great and beautiful city.

From there it is a day's journey to Colo di Bari, which is the great city which King William of Sicily destroyed[33]. Neither Jews nor Gentiles live there at the present day in consequence of its destruction. Thence it is a day and a half to Taranto, which is under the government of Calabria, the inhabitants of which are Greek[34]. It is a large city, and contains about 300 Jews, some of them men of learning, and at their head are R. Meir, R. Nathan, and R. Israel.

From Taranto it is a day's journey to Brindisi, which is on the sea coast. About ten Jews, who are dyers, reside here. It is two days' journey to Otranto, which is on the coast of the Greek sea. Here are about 50 Jews, at the head of them being R. Menachem, R. Caleb, R. Meir, and R. Mali. From Otranto it is a voyage of two days to Corfu, where only one Jew of the name of R. Joseph lives, and here ends the kingdom of Sicily.

Thence it is two days' voyage to the land of Larta (Arta), which is the beginning of the dominions of Emanuel, Sovereign of the Greeks. It is a place containing about 100 Jews, at their head being R. Shelachiah and R. Hercules. From there it is two days to Aphilon (Achelous)[35], a place in which reside about thirty Jews, at their head being R. Sabbattai. From there it takes half a day to Anatolica, which is situated on an arm of the sea [36].

From there it takes a day to Patras, which is the city which Antipater[37], King of the Greeks, built. He was one of the four successors of King Alexander. In the city there are several large old buildings, and about fifty Jews live here, at their head being R. Isaac, R. Jacob, and R. Samuel. Half a day's journey by way of the sea takes one to Kifto (Lepanto)[38], where there are about 100 Jews, who live on the sea-coast; at their head are R. Guri, R. Shallum, and R. Abraham. From there it is a journey of a day and a half to Crissa, where about 200 Jews live apart. They sow and reap on their own land; at their head are R. Solomon, R. Chayim, and R. Jedaiah. From there it is three days' journey to the capital city of Corinth; here are about 300 Jews, at their head being R. Leon, R. Jacob, and R. Hezekiah.

Thence it is two days' journey to the great city of Thebes, where there are about 2,000 Jews. They are the most skilled artificers in silk and purple cloth throughout Greece. They have scholars learned in the Mishnah and the Talmud, and other prominent men, and at their head are the chief rabbi R. Kuti and his brother R. Moses, as well as R. Chiyah, R. Elijah Tirutot, and R. Joktan; and there are none like them in the land of the Greeks, except in the city of Constantinople. From Thebes it is a day's journey to Egripo[39], which is a large city upon the sea-coast, where merchants come from every quarter. About 200 Jews live there, at their head being R. Elijah Psalteri, R. Emanuel, and R. Caleb.

From there it takes a day to Jabustrisa, which is a city upon the sea-coast with about 100 Jews, at their head being R. Joseph, R. Elazar, R. Isaac, R. Samuel, and R. Nethaniah. From there it is a day's journey to Rabonica, where there are about 100 Jews, at their head being R. Joseph, R. Elazar, and R. Isaac.

From there it is a day's journey to Sinon Potamo, where there are about fifty Jews, at their head being R. Solomon and R. Jacob. The city is situated at the foot of the hills of Wallachia. The nation called Wallachians live in those mountains. They are as swift as hinds, and they sweep down from the mountains to despoil and ravage the land of Greece. No man can go up and do battle against them, and no king can rule over them. They do not hold fast to the faith of the Nazarenes, but give themselves Jewish names. Some people say that they are Jews, and, in fact, they call the Jews their brethren, and when they meet with them, though they rob them, they refrain from killing them as they kill the Greeks. They are altogether lawless[40].

From there it is two days' journey to Gardiki, which is in ruins and contains but a few Greeks and Jews. From there it is two days' journey to Armylo, which is a large city on the sea, inhabited by Venetians, Pisans, Genoese, and all the merchants who come there; it is an extensive place, and contains about 400 Jews. At their head are the chief rabbi R. Shiloh Lombardo, R. Joseph, the warden, and R. Solomon, the leading man. Thence it is a day's journey to Vissena, where there are about 100 Jews, at their head being the chief rabbi R. Sabbattai, R. Solomon, and R. Jacob.

From there it is two days' voyage to the city of Salonica, built by King Seleucus, one of the four successors who followed after King Alexander. It is a very large city, with about 500 Jews, including the chief rabbi R. Samuel and his sons, who are scholars. He is appointed by the king as head of the Jews. There is also R. Sabbattai, his son-in-law, R. Elijah, and R. Michael. The Jews are oppressed, and live by silk-weaving.

Thence it is two days' journey to Demetrizi, with about fifty Jews. In this place live R. Isaiah, R. Machir, and R. Alib. Thence it is two days to Drama, where there are about 140 Jews, at the head of them being R. Michael and R. Joseph. From there it is one day's journey to Christopoli, where about twenty Jews live.

A three days' voyage brings one to Abydos, which is upon an arm of the sea which flows between the mountains, and after a five days' journey the great town of Constantinople is reached. It is the capital of the whole land of Javan, which is called Greece. Here is the residence of the King Emanuel the Emperor. Twelve ministers are under him, each of whom has a palace in Constantinople and possesses castles and cities; they rule all the land. At their head is the King Hipparchus, the second in command is the Megas Domesticus, the third Dominus, and the fourth is Megaa Ducas, and the fifth is Oeconomus Megalus; the others bear names like these[41]. The circumference of the city of Constantinople is eighteen miles; half of it is surrounded by the sea, and half by land, and it is situated upon two arms of the sea, one coming from the sea of Russia, and one from the sea of Sepharad.

All sorts of merchants come here from the land of Babylon, from the land of Shinar, from Persia, Media, and all the sovereignty of the land of Egypt, from the land of Canaan, and the empire of Russia[42], from Hungaria, Patzinakia[43], Khazaria[44], and the land of Lombardy and Sepharad. It is a busy city, and merchants come to it from every country by sea or land, and there is none like it in the world except Bagdad, the great city of Islam. In Constantinople is the church of Santa Sophia, and the seat of the Pope of the Greeks, since the Greeks do not obey the Pope of Rome. There are also churches according to the number of the days of the year. A quantity of wealth beyond telling is brought hither year by year as tribute from the two islands and the castles and villages which are there. And the like of this wealth is not to be found in any other church in the world. And in this church there are pillars of gold and silver, and lamps of silver and gold more than a man can count. Close to the walls of the palace is also a place of amusement belonging to the king, which is called the Hippodrome, and every year on the anniversary of the birth of Jesus the king gives a great entertainment there. And in that place men from all the races of the world come before the king and queen with jugglery and without jugglery, and they introduce lions, leopards, bears, and wild asses, and they engage them in combat with one another; and the same thing is done with birds. No entertainment like this is to be found in any other land.

This King Emanuel built a great palace for the seat of his Government upon the sea-coast, in addition to the palaces which his fathers built, and he called its name Blachernae[45]. He overlaid its columns and walls with gold and silver, and engraved thereon representations of the battles before his day and of his own combats. He also set up a throne of gold and of precious stones, and a golden crown was suspended by a gold chain over the throne, so arranged that he might sit thereunder[46]. It was inlaid with jewels of priceless value, and at night time no lights were required, for every one could see by the light which the stones gave forth. Countless other buildings are to be met with in the city. From every part of the empire of Greece tribute is brought here every year, and they fill strongholds with garments of silk, purple, and gold. Like unto these storehouses and this wealth, there is nothing in the whole world to be found. It is said that the tribute of the city amounts every year to 20,000 gold pieces, derived both from the rents of shops and markets, and from the tribute of merchants who enter by sea or land.

The Greek inhabitants are very rich in gold and precious stones, and they go clothed in garments of silk with gold embroidery, and they ride horses, and look like princes. Indeed, the land is very rich in all cloth stuffs, and in bread, meat, and wine. Wealth like that of Constantinople is not to be found in the whole world. Here also are men learned in all the books of the Greeks, and they eat and drink every man under his vine and his fig-tree.

They hire from amongst all nations warriors called Loazim (Barbarians) to fight with the Sultan Masud[47], King of the Togarmim (Seljuks), who are called Turks; for the natives are not warlike, but are as women who have no strength to fight.

No Jews live in the city, for they have been placed behind an inlet of the sea. An arm of the sea of Marmora shuts them in on the one side, and they are unable to go out except by way of the sea, when they want to do business with the inhabitants[48]. In the Jewish quarter are about 2,000 Rabbanite Jews and about 500 Karaïtes, and a fence divides them. Amongst the scholars are several wise men, at their head being the chief rabbi R. Abtalion, R. Obadiah, R. Aaron Bechor Shoro, R. Joseph Shir-Guru, and R. Eliakim, the warden. And amongst them there are artificers in silk and many rich merchants. No Jew there is allowed to ride on horseback. The one exception is R. Solomon Hamitsri, who is the king's physician, and through whom the Jews enjoy considerable alleviation of their oppression. For their condition is very low, and there is much hatred against them, which is fostered by the tanners, who throw out their dirty water in the streets before the doors of the Jewish houses and defile the Jews' quarter (the Ghetto). So the Greeks hate the Jews, good and bad alike, and subject them to great oppression, and beat them in the streets, and in every way treat them with rigour. Yet the Jews are rich and good, kindly and charitable, and bear their lot with cheerfulness. The district inhabited by the Jews is called Pera.

From Constantinople it is two days' voyage to Rhaedestus[49], with a community of Israelites of about 400, at their head being R. Moses, R. Abijah, and R. Jacob. From there it is two days to Callipolis (Gallipoli), where there are about 200 Jews, at their head being R. Elijah Kapur, R. Shabbattai Zutro, and R. Isaac Megas, which means "great" in Greek. And from here it is two days to Kales. Here there are about fifty Jews, at their head being R. Jacob and R. Judah. From here it is two days' journey to the island of Mytilene, and there are Jewish congregations in ten localities on the island. Thence it is three days' voyage to the island of Chios, where there are about 400 Jews, including R. Elijah Heman and R. Shabtha. Here grow the trees from which mastic is obtained. Two days' voyage takes one to the island of Samos, where there are 300 Jews, at their head being R. Shemaria, R. Obadiah, and R. Joel. The islands have many congregations of Jews. From Samos it is three days to Rhodes, where there are about 400 Jews, at their head being R. Abba, R. Hannanel, and R. Elijah. It is four days' voyage from here to Cyprus, where there are Rabbanite Jews and Karaïtes; there are also some heretical Jews called Epikursin, whom the Israelites have excommunicated in all places. They profane the eve of the sabbath, and observe the first night of the week, which is the termination of the sabbath[50]. From Cyprus it is four days' journey to Curicus (Kurch), which is the beginning of the land called Armenia, and this is the frontier of the empire of Thoros[51], ruler of the mountains, and king of Armenia, whose dominions extend to the province of Trunia[52], and to the country of the Togarmim or Turks. From there it is two days' journey to Malmistras, which is Tarshish, situated by the sea; and thus far extends the kingdom of the Javanim or Greeks[53].

Thence it is two days' journey to Antioch the Great, situated on the river Fur (Orontes), which is the river Jabbok, that flows from Mount

Lebanon and from the land of Hamath[54]. This is the great city which Antiochus the king built. The city lies by a lofty mountain, which is surrounded by the city-wall. At the top of the mountain is a well, from which a man appointed for that purpose directs the water by means of twenty subterranean passages to the houses of the great men of the city. The other part of the city is surrounded by the river. It is a strongly fortified city, and is under the sway of Prince Boemond Poitevin[55], surnamed le Baube. Ten Jews[56] dwell here, engaged in glass-making, and at their head are R. Mordecai, R. Chayim, and R. Samuel. From here it is two days' journey to Lega, or Ladikiya, where there are about 100 Jews, at their head being R. Chayim and R. Joseph.

Thence it is two days' journey to Gebal (Gebela), which is Baal-Gad, at the foot of Lebanon[57]. In the neighbourhood dwells a people called Al-Hashishim[58]. They do not believe in the religion of Islam, but follow one of their own folk, whom they regard as their prophet, and all that he tells them to do they carry out, whether for death or life. They call him the Sheik Al Hashishim, and he is known as their Elder. At his word these mountaineers go out and come in. Their principal seat is Kadmus, which is Kedemoth in the land of Sihon. They are faithful to each other, but a source of terror to their neighbours, killing even kings at the cost of their own lives. The extent of their land is eight days' journey. And they are at war with the sons of Edom who are called the Franks, and with the ruler of Tripolis, which is Tarabulus el Sham[59]. At Tripolis in years gone by there was an earthquake, when many Gentiles and Jews perished, for houses and walls fell upon them. There was great destruction at that time throughout the Land of Israel, and more than 20,000 souls perished[60].

Thence it is a day's journey to the other Gebal (Gubail), which borders on the land of the children of Ammon, and here there are about 150 Jews. The place is under the rule of the Genoese, the name of the governor being Guillelmus Embriacus[61]. Here was found a temple belonging to the children of Ammon in olden times, and an idol of theirs seated upon a throne or chair, and made of stone overlaid with gold. Two women are represented sitting one on the right and one on the left of it, and there is an altar in front before which the Ammonites used to sacrifice and burn incense[62]. There are about 200 Jews there, at their head being R. Meir, R. Jacob, and R. Simchah. The place is situated on the sea-border of the land of Israel. From there it is two days' journey to Beirut, or Beeroth, where there are about fifty Jews, at their head being R. Solomon, R. Obadiah, and R. Joseph. Thence it is one day's journey to Saida, which is Sidon, a large city, with about twenty Jews. Ten miles therefrom a people dwell who are at war with the men of Sidon; they are called Druses, and are pagans of a lawless character. They inhabit the mountains and the clefts of the rocks; they have no king or ruler, but dwell independent in these high places, and their border extends to Mount Hermon, which is a three days' journey. They are steeped in vice, brothers marrying their sisters, and fathers their daughters. They have one feast-day in the year, when they all collect, both men and women, to eat and drink together, and they then interchange their wives[63]. They say that at the time when the soul leaves the body it passes in the case of a good man into the body of a newborn child, and in the case of a bad man into the body of a dog or an ass. Such are their foolish beliefs. There are no resident Jews among them, but a certain number of Jewish handicraftsmen and dyers come among them for the sake of trade, and then return, the people being favourable to the Jews. They roam over the mountains and hills, and no man can do battle with them.

From Sidon it is half a day's journey to Sarepta (Sarfend), which belongs to Sidon. Thence it is a half-day to New Tyre (Sŭr), which is a very fine city, with a harbour in its midst. At night-time those that levy dues throw iron chains from tower to tower, so that no man can go forth by boat or in any other way to rob the ships by night. There is no harbour like this in the whole world. Tyre is a beautiful city. It contains about 500 Jews, some of them scholars of the Talmud, at their head being R. Ephraim of Tyre, the Dayan, R. Meir from Carcassonne, and R. Abraham, head of the congregation. The Jews own sea-going vessels, and there are glass-makers amongst them who make that fine Tyrian glass-ware which is prized in all countries.

In the vicinity is found sugar of a high class, for men plant it here, and people come from all lands to buy it[64]. A man can ascend the walls of New Tyre and see ancient Tyre, which the sea has now covered, lying at a stone's throw from the new city. And should one care to go forth by boat, one can see the castles, market-places, streets, and palaces in the bed of the sea. New Tyre is a busy place of commerce, to which merchants flock from all quarters.

One day's journey brings one to Acre, the Acco of old, which is on the borders of Asher; it is the commencement of the land of Israel. Situated by the Great Sea, it possesses a large harbour for all the pilgrims who come to Jerusalem by ship. A stream runs in front of it, called the brook of Kedumim[65]. About 200 Jews live there, at their head being R. Zadok, R. Japheth, and R. Jonah. From there it is three parasangs to Haifa, which is Hahepher[66] on the seaboard, and on the other side is Mount Carmel[67], at the foot of which there are many Jewish graves. On the mountain is the cave of Elijah, where the Christians have erected a structure called St. Elias. On the top of the mountain can be recognized the overthrown altar which Elijah repaired in the days of Ahab. The site of the altar is circular, about four cubits remain thereof, and at the foot of the mountain the brook Kishon flows. From here it is four parasangs to Capernaum, which is the village of Nahum, identical with Maon, the home of Nabal the Carmelite[68].

Six parasangs from here is Caesarea, the Gath[69] of the Philistines, and here there are about 200 Jews and 200 Cuthim. These are the Jews of Shomron, who are called Samaritans. The city is fair and beautiful, and lies by the sea. It was built by Caesar, and called after him Caesarea. Thence it is half a day's journey to Kako[70], the Keilah of Scripture. There are no Jews here. Thence it is half a day's journey to St. George, which is Ludd[71], where there lives one Jew, who is a dyer. Thence it is a day's journey to Sebastiya, which is the city of Shomron (Samaria), and here the ruins of the palace of Ahab the son of Omri may be seen. It was formerly a well-fortified city by the mountain-side, with streams of water. It is still a land of brooks of water, gardens, orchards, vineyards, and olive groves, but no Jews dwell here. Thence it is two parasangs to Nablous, which is Shechem on Mount Ephraim, where there are no Jews; the place is situated in the valley between Mount Gerizim and Mount Ebal, and contains about 1,000 Cuthim, who observe the written law of Moses alone, and are called Samaritans. They have priests of the seed (of Aaron), and they call them Aaronim, who do not intermarry with Cuthim, but wed only amongst themselves[72]. These priests offer sacrifices, and bring burnt-offerings in their place of assembly on Mount Gerizim, as it is written in their law—"And thou shalt set the blessing on Mount Gerizim." They say that this is the proper site of the Temple. On Passover and the other festivals they offer up burnt-offerings on the altar which they have built on Mount Gerizim, as it is written in their law—"Ye shall set up the stones upon Mount Gerizim, of the stones which Joshua and the children of Israel set up at the Jordan." They say that they are descended from the tribe of Ephraim. And in the midst of them is the grave of Joseph, the son of Jacob our father, as it is written— "and the bones of Joseph buried they in Shechem[73]." Their alphabet lacks three letters, namely ה He, ח Heth, and ע Ain [74]. The letter ה He is taken from Abraham our father, because they have no dignity, the letter ח Heth from Isaac, because they have no kindliness, and the letter ע Ain from Jacob, because they have no humility. In place of these letters they make use of the Aleph, by which we can tell that they are not of the seed of Israel, although they know the law of Moses with the exception of these three letters. They guard themselves from the defilement of the dead, of the bones of the slain, and of graves; and they remove the garments which they have worn before they go to the place of worship, and they bathe and put on fresh clothes. This is their constant practice. On Mount Gerizim are fountains and gardens and plantations, but Mount

Ebal is rocky and barren; and between them in the valley lies the city of Shechem.

From the latter place it is a distance of four parasangs to Mount Gilboa, which the Christians call Mont Gilboa; it lies in a very parched district. And from there it is five[75] . . ., a village where there are no Jews. Thence it is two parasangs to the valley of Ajalon[76], which the Christians call Val-de-Luna. At a distance of one parasang is Mahomerie-le-Grand, which is Gibeon the Great; it contains no Jews.

From there it is three parasangs to Jerusalem, which is a small city, fortified by three walls. It is full of people whom the Mohammedans call Jacobites, Syrians, Greeks, Georgians and Franks, and of people of all tongues. It contains a dyeing-house, for which the Jews pay a small rent annually to the king[77], on condition that besides the Jews no other dyers be allowed in Jerusalem. There are about 200 Jews who dwell under the Tower of David in one corner of the city[78]. The lower portion of the wall of the Tower of David, to the extent of about ten cubits, is part of the ancient foundation set up by our ancestors, the remaining portion having been built by the Mohammedans. There is no structure in the whole city stronger than the Tower of David. The city also contains two buildings, from one of which—the hospital—there issue forth four hundred knights; and therein all the sick who come thither are lodged and cared for in life and in death[79]. The other building is called the Temple of Solomon; it is the palace built by Solomon the king of Israel. Three hundred knights are quartered there, and issue therefrom every day for military exercise, besides those who come from the land of the Franks and the other parts of Christendom, having taken upon themselves to serve there a year or two until their vow is fulfilled. In Jerusalem is the great church called the Sepulchre, and here is the burial-place of Jesus, unto which the Christians make pilgrimages.[

Jerusalem[80] has four gates—the gate of Abraham, the gate of David, the gate of Zion, and the gate of Gushpat, which is the gate of Jehoshaphat, facing our ancient Temple, now called Templum Domini.

Upon the site of the sanctuary Omar ben al Khataab erected an edifice with a very large and magnificent cupola, into which the Gentiles do not bring any image or effigy, but they merely come there to pray. In front of this place is the western wall, which is one of the walls of the Holy of Holies. This is called the Gate of Mercy, and thither come all the Jews to pray before the wall of the court of the Temple. In Jerusalem, attached to the palace which belonged to Solomon, are the stables built by him, forming a very substantial structure, composed of large stones, and the like of it is not to be seen anywhere in the world. There is also visible up to this day the pool used by the priests before offering their sacrifices, and the Jews coming thither write their names upon the wall. The gate of Jehoshaphat leads to the valley of Jehoshaphat, which is the gathering-place of nations[81]. Here is the pillar called Absalom's Hand, and the sepulchre of King Uzziah[82].

In the neighbourhood is also a great spring, called the Waters of Siloam, connected with the brook of Kidron. Over the spring is a large structure dating from the time of our ancestors, but little water is found, and the people of Jerusalem for the most part drink the rain-water, which they collect in cisterns in their houses. From the valley of Jehoshaphat one ascends the Mount of Olives; it is the valley only which separates Jerusalem from the Mount of Olives. From the Mount of Olives one sees the Sea of Sodom, and at a distance of two parasangs from the Sea of Sodom is the Pillar of Salt into which Lot's wife was turned; the sheep lick it continually, but afterwards it regains its original shape[83]. The whole land of the plain and the valley of Shittim as far as Mount Nebo are visible from here.

In front of Jerusalem is Mount Zion, on which there is no building, except a place of worship belonging to the Christians. Facing Jerusalem for a distance of three miles are the cemeteries[84] belonging to the Israelites, who in the days of old buried their dead in caves, and upon each sepulchre is a dated inscription, but the Christians destroy the sepulchres, employing the stones thereof in building their houses. These sepulchres reach as far as Zelzah in the territory of Benjamin. Around Jerusalem are high mountains.

On Mount Zion are the sepulchres of the House of David, and the sepulchres of the kings that ruled after him. The exact place cannot be identified, inasmuch as fifteen years ago a wall of the church of Mount Zion fell in. The Patriarch commanded the overseer to take the stones of the old walls and restore therewith the church. He did so, and hired workmen at fixed wages; and there were twenty men who brought the stones from the base of the wall of Zion. Among these men there were two who were sworn friends. On a certain day the one entertained the other; after their meal they returned to their work, when the overseer said to them, "Why have you tarried to-day?" They answered, "Why need you complain? When our fellow workmen go to their meal we will do our work." When the dinner-time arrived, and the other workmen had gone to their meal, they examined the stones, and raised a certain stone which formed the entrance to a cave. Thereupon one said to the other, "Let us go in and see if any money is to be found there." They entered the cave, and reached a large chamber resting upon pillars of marble overlaid with silver and gold. In front was a table of gold and a sceptre and crown. This was the sepulchre of King David. On the left thereof in like fashion was the sepulchre of King Solomon; then followed the sepulchres of all the kings of Judah that were buried there. Closed coffers were also there, the contents of which no man knows. The two men essayed to enter the chamber, when a fierce wind came forth from the entrance of the cave and smote them, and they fell to the ground like dead men, and there they lay until evening. And there came forth a wind like a man's voice, crying out: "Arise and go forth from this place!" So the men rushed forth in terror, and they came unto the Patriarch, and related these things to him. Thereupon the Patriarch sent for Rabbi Abraham el Constantini, the pious recluse, who was one of the mourners of Jerusalem, and to him he related all these things according to the report of the two men who had come forth. Then Rabbi Abraham replied, "These are the sepulchres of the House of David; they belong to the kings of Judah, and on the morrow let us enter. I and you and these men, and find out what is there." And on the morrow they sent for the two men, and found each of them lying on his bed in terror, and the men said: "We will not enter there, for the Lord doth not desire to show it to any man." Then the Patriarch gave orders that the place should be closed up and hidden from the sight of man unto this day. These things were told me by the said Rabbi Abraham.

From Jerusalem it is two parasangs to Bethlehem, which is called by the Christians Beth-Leon, and close thereto, at a distance of about half a mile, at the parting of the way, is the pillar of Rachel's grave, which is made up of eleven stones, corresponding with the number of the sons of Jacob. Upon it is a cupola resting on four columns, and all the Jews that pass by carve their names upon the stones of the pillar[85]. At Bethlehem there are two Jewish dyers. It is a land of brooks of water, and contains wells and fountains.

At a distance of six parasangs is St. Abram de Bron, which is Hebron; the old city stood on the mountain, but is now in ruins; and in the valley by the field of Machpelah lies the present city. Here there is the great church called St. Abram, and this was a Jewish place of worship at the time of the Mohammedan rule, but the Gentiles have erected there six tombs, respectively called those of Abraham and Sarah, Isaac and Rebekah, Jacob and Leah. The custodians tell the pilgrims that these are the tombs of the Patriarchs, for which information the pilgrims give them money. If a Jew comes, however, and gives a special reward, the custodian of the cave opens unto him a gate of iron, which was constructed by our forefathers, and then he is able to descend below by means of steps, holding a lighted candle in his hand. He then reaches a cave, in which nothing is to be found, and a cave beyond, which is likewise empty, but when he reaches the third cave behold there are six sepulchres, those of Abraham, Isaac and Jacob, respectively facing those of Sarah, Rebekah and Leah. And upon the graves are inscriptions cut in stone; upon the grave of Abraham is engraved "This is the grave of Abraham"; upon that of Isaac, "This is the grave of Isaac, the son of Abraham our Father"; upon that of Jacob, "This is the grave of Jacob, the son of Isaac, the son of Abraham our Father"; and upon the others, "This is the grave of Sarah," "This is the grave of Rebekah," and "This is the grave of Leah." A lamp burns day and night upon the graves in the cave.

One finds there many casks filled with the bones of Israelites, as the members of the house of Israel were wont to bring the bones of their fathers thither and to deposit them there to this day[86].

Beyond the field of Machpelah is the house of Abraham; there is a well in front of the house, but out of reverence for the Patriarch Abraham no one is allowed to build in the neighbourhood.

From Hebron it is five parasangs to Beit Jibrin, which is Mareshah, where there are but three Jews[87]. Three parasangs further one reaches St. Samuel of Shiloh. This is the Shiloh which is two parasangs from Jerusalem. When the Christians captured Ramlah, the Ramah of old, from the Mohammedans, they found there the grave of Samuel the Ramathite close to a Jewish synagogue. The Christians took the remains, conveyed them unto Shiloh, and erected over them a large church, and called it St. Samuel of Shiloh unto this day[88].

From there it is three parasangs to Mahomerie-le-petit[89], which is Gibeah of Saul, where there are no Jews, and this is Gibeah of Benjamin. Thence three parasangs to Beit Nuba[90], which is Nob, the city of priests. In the middle of the way are the two crags of Jonathan, the name of the one being Bozez, and the name of the other Seneh[91]. Two Jewish dyers dwell there.

Thence it is three parasangs to Rams, or Ramleh, where there are remains of the walls from the days of our ancestors, for thus it was found written upon the stones. About 300 Jews dwell there. It was formerly a very great city; at a distance of two miles there is a large Jewish cemetery[92].

Thence it is five parasangs to Yâfa or Jaffa, which is on the seaboard, and one Jewish dyer lives here. From here it is five parasangs to Ibelin or

Jabneh, the seat of the Academy, but there are no Jews there at this day. Thus far extends the territory of Ephraim.

From there it is five parasangs to Palmid, which is Ashdod of the Philistines, now in ruins; no Jews dwell there. Thence it is two parasangs to Ashkelonah or New Askelon, which Ezra the priest built by the sea. It was originally called Bene Berak. The place is four parasangs distant from the ancient ruined city of Askelon. New Askelon is a large and fair place, and merchants come thither from all quarters, for it is situated on the frontier of Egypt. About 200 Rabbanite Jews dwell here, at their head being R. Zemach, R. Aaron, and R. Solomon; also about forty Karaïtes, and about 300 Cuthim. In the midst of the city there is a well, which they call Bir Abraham; this the Patriarch dug in the days of the Philistines[93].

From there it is a journey of a day to St. George[94] of Ludd: thence it is a day and a half to Zerin or Jezreel, where there is a large spring. One Jewish dyer lives here. Three parasangs further is Saffuriya or Sepphoris. Here are the graves of Rabbenu Hakkadosh, of Rabban Gamaliel, and of R. Chiya, who came up from Babylon, also of Jonah the son of Amittai; they are all buried in the mountain[95]. Many other Jewish graves are here.

Thence it is five parasangs to Tiberias, which is situated upon the Jordan, which is here called the Sea of Chinnereth. The Jordan at this place flows through a valley between two mountains, and fills the lake, which is called the Lake of Chinnereth; this is a large and broad piece of water like the sea. The Jordan flows between two mountains, and over the plain which is the place that is called Ashdoth Hapisgah, and thence continues its course till it falls into the Sea of Sodom, which is the Salt Sea. In Tiberias there are about fifty Jews, at their head being R. Abraham the astronomer, R. Muchtar, and R. Isaac. There are hot waters here, which bubble up from the ground, and are called the Hot Waters of Tiberias. Near by is the Synagogue of Caleb ben Jephunneh, and Jewish sepulchres. R. Johanan ben Zakkai and R. Jehudah Halevi[96] are buried here. All these places are situated in Lower Galilee.

From here it is two days to Tymin or Timnathah, where Simon the Just[97] and many Israelites are buried, and thence three parasangs to Medon or Meron. In the neighbourhood there is a cave in which are the sepulchres of Hillel and Shammai. Here also are twenty sepulchres of disciples, including the sepulchres of R. Benjamin ben Japheth, and of R. Jehudah ben Bethera. From Meron it is two parasangs to Almah, where there are about fifty Jews. There is a large Jewish cemetery here, with the sepulchres of R. Eleazar ben Arak, of R. Eleazar ben Azariah, of Chuni Hamaagal, of Raban Simeon ben Gamaliel, and of R. Jose Hagelili[98].

From here it is half a day's journey to Kades, or Kedesh Naphtali, upon the Jordan. Here is the sepulchre of Barak the son of Abinoam. No Jews dwell here.

Thence it is a day's journey to Banias, which is Dan, where there is a cavern, from which the Jordan issues and flows for a distance of three miles, when the Arnon, which comes from the borders of Moab, joins it[99]. In front of the cavern may be discerned the site of the altar associated with the graven image of Micah, which the children of Dan worshipped in ancient days. This is also the site of the altar of Jeroboam, where the golden calf was set up. Thus far reaches the boundary of the land of Israel towards the uttermost sea[100].

Two days' journey brings one to Damascus, the great city, which is the commencement of the empire of Nur-ed-din, the king of the Togarmim, called Turks. It is a fair city of large extent, surrounded by walls, with many gardens and plantations, extending over fifteen miles on each side, and no district richer in fruit can be seen in all the world. From Mount Hermon descend the rivers Amana and Pharpar; for the city is situated at the foot of Mount Hermon. The Amana flows through the city, and by means of aqueducts the water is conveyed to the houses of the great people, and into the streets and market-places. The Pharpar flows through their gardens and plantations. It is a place carrying on trade with all countries. Here is a mosque of the Arabs called the Gami of Damascus; there is no building like it in the whole world, and they say that it was a palace of

Ben Hadad. Here is a wall of crystal glass of magic workmanship, with apertures according to the days of the year, and as the sun's rays enter each of them in daily succession the hours of the day can be told by a graduated dial. In the palace are chambers built of gold and glass, and if people walk round the wall they are able to see one another, although the wall is between them. And there are columns overlaid with gold and silver, and columns of marble of all colours[101]. And in the court there is a gigantic head overlaid with gold and silver, and fashioned like a bowl with rims of gold and silver. It is as big as a cask, and three men can enter therein at the same time to bathe. In the palace is suspended the rib of one of the giants, the length being nine cubits, and the width two cubits; and they say it belonged to the King Anak of the giants of old, whose name was Abramaz[102]. For so it was found inscribed on his grave, where it was also written that he ruled over the whole world. Three thousand Jews abide in this city, and amongst them are learned and rich men[103]. The head of the Academy of the land of Israel resides here[104]. His name is R. Azariah, and with him are his brother, Sar Shalom, the head of the Beth Din: R. Joseph, the fifth of the Academy: R. Mazliach, the lecturer, the head of the order: R. Meir, the crown of the scholars: R. Joseph ben Al Pilath, the pillar of the Academy: R. Heman, the warden: and R. Zedekiah, the physician. One hundred Karaïtes dwell here, also 400 Cuthim, and there is peace between them, but they do not intermarry.

It is a day's journey to Galid, which is Gilead, and sixty Israelites are there, at their head being R. Zadok, R. Isaac, and R. Solomon. It is a place of wide extent, with brooks of water, gardens, and plantations. Thence it is half a day to Salkat, which is Salchah of old[105].

Thence it is half a day's journey to Baalbec, which is Baalath in the plains of Lebanon, and which Solomon built for the daughter of Pharaoh. The palace is built of large stones, each stone having a length of twenty cubits and a width of twelve cubits, and there are no spaces between the stones. It is said that Ashmedai alone could have put up this building. From the upper part of the city a great spring wells forth and flows into the middle of the city as a wide stream, and alongside thereof are mills and gardens and plantations in the midst of the city. At Tarmod (Tadmor) in the wilderness, which Solomon built, there are similar structures of huge stones.[106] The city of Tarmod is surrounded by walls; it is in the desert far away from inhabited places, and is four days' journey from Baalath, just mentioned. And in Tarmod there are about 2,000 Jews. They are valiant in war and fight with the Christians and with the Arabs, which latter are under the dominion of Nur-ed-din the king, and they help their neighbours the Ishmaelites. At their head are R. Isaac Hajvani, R. Nathan, and R. Uziel.

From Baalbec to Karjatîn, which 1s Kirjathim, is a distance of half a day; no Jews live there except one dyer. Thence it is a day's journey to Emesa, which is a city of the Zemarites, where about twenty Jews dwell[107]. Thence it is a day's journey to Hamah, which is Hamath. It lies on the river Jabbok at the foot of Mount Lebanon[108]. Some time ago there was a great earthquake in the city, and 25,000 souls perished in one day, and of about 200 Jews but seventy escaped. At their head are R. Eli Hacohen, and the Sheik Abu Galib and Mukhtar. Thence it is half a day to Sheizar, which is Hazor[109], and from there it is three parasangs to Dimin (Latmin).

Thence it is two days to Haleb (Aleppo) or Aram Zoba, which is the royal city of Nur-ed-din. In the midst of the city is his palace surrounded by a very high wall. This is a very large place. There is no well there nor any stream, but the inhabitants drink rainwater, each one possessing a cistern in his house[110]. The city has 5,000 Jewish inhabitants, at their head being R. Moses el Constantini and R. Seth. Thence it is two days to Balis[111], which is Pethor on the river Euphrates, and unto this day there stands the turret of Balaam, which he built to tell the hours of the day. About ten Jews live here. Thence it is half a day to Kalat Jabar, which is Selah of the wilderness, that was left unto the Arabs at the time the Togarmim took their land and caused them to fly into the wilderness.

About 2,000 Jews dwell there, at their head being R. Zedekiah, R. Chiya, and R. Solomon.

Thence it is one day's journey to Rakka[112], or Salchah, which is on the confines of the land of Shinar, and which divides the land of the Togarmim from that kingdom. In it there are 700 Jews, at their head being R. Zakkai and R. Nedib, who is blind, and R. Joseph. There is a synagogue here, erected by Ezra when he went forth from Babylon to Jerusalem. At two days' distance lies ancient Harrân, where twenty Jews live[113]. Here is another synagogue erected by Ezra, and in this place stood the house of Terah and Abraham his son. The ground is not covered by any building, and the Mohammedans honour the site and come thither to pray.

Thence it is a journey of two days to Ras-el-Ain[114], whence proceeds the river El Khabur—the Habor of old—which flows through the land of Media, and falls into the river Gozan[115]. Here there are 200 Jews[116]. Thence it is two days to Geziret Ibn Omar, which is surrounded by the river Hiddekel (Tigris), at the foot of the mountains of Ararat.

It is a distance of four miles to the place where Noah's Ark rested, but Omar ben al Khataab took the ark from the two mountains and made it into a mosque for the Mohammedans[117]. Near the ark is the Synagogue of Ezra to this day, and on the ninth of Ab the Jews come thither from the city to pray. In the city of Geziret Omar are 4,000 Jews, at their head being R. Mubchar, R. Joseph and R. Chiya.

Thence it is two days to Mosul, which is Assur the Great, and here dwell about 7,000 Jews, at their head being R. Zakkai the Nasi of the seed of David, and R. Joseph surnamed Burhan-al-mulk, the astronomer to the King Sin-ed-din, the brother of Nur-ed-din, King of Damascus[118]. Mosul is the frontier town of the land of Persia.

It is a very large and ancient city, situated on the river Hiddekel (Tigris), and is connected with Nineveh by means of a bridge. Nineveh is in ruins, but amid the ruins there are villages and hamlets, and the extent of the city may be determined by the walls, which extend forty parasangs to the city of Irbil[119]. The city of Nineveh is on the river Hiddekel. In the city of Assur (Mosul) is the synagogue of Obadiah, built by Jonah; also the synagogue of Nahum the Elkoshite[120].

Thence it is a distance of three days to Rahbah, which is on the river Euphrates. Here there are about 2,000 Jews, at their head being R. Hezekiah, R. Tahor and R. Isaac. It is a very fine city, large and fortified, and surrounded by gardens and plantations.

Thence it is a day's journey to Karkisiya which is Carchemish, on the river Euphrates. Here there are about 500 Jews, at their head being R. Isaac and R. Elhanan. Thence it is two days to El-Anbar which is Pumbedita in Nehardea[121]. Here reside 3,000 Jews, and amongst them are learned men, at their head being the chief rabbi R. Chen, R. Moses and R. Jehoiakim. Here are the graves of Rab Jehuda and Samuel, and in front of the graves of each of them are the synagogues which they built in their lifetime. Here is also the grave of Bostanai the Nasi, the head of the Captivity, and of R. Nathan and Rab Nachman the son of Papa.

Thence it takes five days to Hadara, where about 15,000 Jews dwell, at their head being R. Zaken, R. Jehosef and R. Nethanel[122].

Thence it takes two days to Okbara, the city, which Jeconiah the King built, where there are about 10,000 Jews, and at their head are R. Chanan, R. Jabin and R. Ishmael.

Thence it is two days to Bagdad, the great city and the royal residence of the Caliph Emir al Muminin al Abbasi of the family of Mohammed. He is at the head of the Mohammedan religion, and all the kings of Islam obey him; he occupies a similar position to that held by the Pope over the Christians[123]. He has a palace in Bagdad three miles in extent, wherein is a great park with all varieties of trees, fruit-bearing and otherwise, and all manner of animals. The whole is surrounded by a wall, and in the park there is a lake whose waters are fed by the river Hiddekel. Whenever the king desires to indulge in recreation and to rejoice and feast, his servants catch all manner of birds, game and fish, and he goes to his palace with his counsellors and princes. There the great king, Al Abbasi the Caliph

(Hafiz) holds his court, and he is kind unto Israel, and many belonging to the people of Israel are his attendants; he knows all languages, and is well versed in the law of Israel. He reads and writes the holy language (Hebrew). He will not partake of anything unless he has earned it by the work of his own hands. He makes coverlets to which he attaches his seal; his courtiers sell them in the market, and the great ones of the land purchase them, and the proceeds thereof provide his sustenance. He is truthful and trusty, speaking peace to all men. The men of Islam see him but once in the year. The pilgrims that come from distant lands to go unto Mecca which is in the land El-Yemen, are anxious to see his face, and they assemble before the palace exclaiming "Our Lord, light of Islam and glory of our Law, show us the effulgence of thy countenance," but he pays no regard to their words. Then the princes who minister unto him say to him, "Our Lord, spread forth thy peace unto the men that have come from distant lands, who crave to abide under the shadow of thy graciousness," and thereupon he arises and lets down the hem of his robe from the window, and the pilgrims come and kiss it[124], and a prince says unto them "Go forth in peace, for our Master the Lord of Islam granteth peace to you." He is regarded by them as Mohammed and they go to their houses rejoicing at the salutation which the prince has vouchsafed unto them, and glad at heart that they have kissed his robe.

Each of his brothers and the members of his family has an abode in his palace, but they are all fettered in chains of iron, and guards are placed over each of their houses so that they may not rise against the great Caliph. For once it happened to a predecessor that his brothers rose up against him and proclaimed one of themselves as Caliph; then it was decreed that all the members of his family should be bound, that they might not rise up against the ruling Caliph. Each one of them resides in his palace in great splendour, and they own villages and towns, and their stewards bring them the tribute thereof, and they eat and drink and rejoice all the days of their life[125]. Within the domains of the palace of the Caliph there are great buildings of marble and columns of silver and gold, andp. 57

carvings upon rare stones are fixed in the walls. In the Caliph's palace are great riches and towers filled with gold, silken garments and all precious stones. He does not issue forth from his palace save once in the year, at the feast which the Mohammedans call El-id-bed Ramazan, and they come from distant lands that day to see him. He rides on a mule and is attired in the royal robes of gold and silver and fine linen; on his head is a turban adorned with precious stones of priceless value, and over the turban is a black shawl as a sign of his modesty, implying that all this glory will be covered by darkness on the day of death. He is accompanied by all the nobles of Islam dressed in fine garments and riding on horses, the princes of Arabia, the princes of Togarma and Daylam (Gilân) and the princes of Persia, Media and Ghuzz, and the princes of the land of Tibet, which is three months' journey distant, and westward of which lies the land of Samarkand. He proceeds from his palace to the great mosque of Islam which is by the Basrah Gate. Along the road the walls are adorned with silk and purple, and the inhabitants receive him with all kinds of song and exultation, and they dance before the great king who is styled the Caliph. They salute him with a loud voice and say, "Peace unto thee, our Lord the King and Light of Islam!" He kisses his robe, and stretching forth the hem thereof he salutes them. Then he proceeds to the court of the mosque, mounts a wooden pulpit and expounds to them their Law. Then the learned ones of Islam arise and pray for him and extol his greatness and his graciousness, to which they all respond. Afterwards he gives them his blessing, and they bring before him a camel which he slays, and this is their passover-sacrifice. He gives thereof unto the princes and they distribute it to all, so that they may taste of the sacrifice brought by their sacred king; and they all rejoice. Afterwards he leaves the mosque and returns alone to his palace by way of the river Hiddekel, and the grandees of Islam accompany him in ships on the river until he enters his palace. He does not return the way he came; and the road which he takes along the river-side is watched all the year through, so that no man shall tread in his footsteps. He does not leave the palace again for a whole year. He is a benevolent man.

He built, on the other side of the river, on the banks of an arm of theEuphrates which there borders the city, a hospital consisting of blocks of houses and hospices for the sick poor who come to be healed[126]. Here there are about sixty physicians' stores which are provided from the Caliph's house with drugs and whatever else may be required. Every sick man who comes is maintained at the Caliph's expense and is medically treated. Here is a building which is called Dar-al-Maristan, where they keep charge of the demented people who have become insane in the towns through the great heat in the summer, and they chain each of them in iron chains until their reason becomes restored to them in the winter-time. Whilst they abide there, they are provided with food from the house of the Caliph, and when their reason is restored they are dismissed and each one of them goes to his house and his home. Money is given to those that have stayed in the hospices on their return to their homes. Every month the officers of the Caliph inquire and investigate whether they have regained their reason, in which case they are discharged. All this the Caliph does out of charity to those that come to the city of Bagdad, whether they be sick or insane. The Caliph is a righteous man, and all his actions are for good.

In Bagdad there are about 40,000 Jews[127], and they dwell in security, prosperity and honour under the great Caliph, and amongst them are great sages, the heads of Academies engaged in the study of the law. In this city there are ten Academies. At the head of the great Academy is the chief rabbi R. Samuel, the son of Eli. He is the head of the Academy Gaon Jacob. He is a Levite, and traces his pedigree back to Moses our teacher. The head of the second Academy is R. Hanania his brother, warden of the Levites; R. Daniel is the head of the third Academy; R. Elazar the scholar is the head of the fourth Academy; and R. Elazar, the son of Zemach, is the head of the order, and his pedigree reaches to Samuel the prophet, the Korahite. He and his brethren know how to chant the melodies as did the singers at the time when the Temple was standing. He is head of the fifth Academy. R. Hisdai, the glory of the scholars, is head of the sixth Academy. R. Haggai is head of the seventh Academy. R. Ezra is the head of the eighth Academy. R. Abraham, who is called Abu Tahir, is the head of the ninth Academy. R. Zakkai, the son of Bostanai the Nasi, is the head of the Sium[128]. These are the ten Batlanim[129], and they do not engage in any other work than communal administration; and all the days of the week they judge the Jews their countrymen, except on the second day of the week, when they all appear before the chief rabbi Samuel, the head of the Yeshiba Gaon (Jacob), who in conjunction with the other Batlanim judges all those that appear before him. And at the head of them all is Daniel the son of Hisdai, who is styled "Our Lord the Head of the Captivity of all Israel." He possesses a book of pedigrees going back as far as David, King of Israel. The Jews call him "Our Lord, Head of the Captivity," and the Mohammedans call him "Saidna ben Daoud," and he has been invested with authority over all the congregations of Israel at the hands of the Emir al Muminin, the Lord of Islam[130].

For thus Mohammed commanded concerning him and his descendants; and he granted him a seal of office over all the congregations that dwell under his rule, and ordered that every one, whether Mohammedan or Jew, or belonging to any other nation in his dominion, should rise up before him (the Exilarch) and salute him, and that any one who should refuse to rise up should receive one hundred stripes[131].

And every fifth day when he goes to pay a visit to the great Caliph, horsemen, Gentiles as well as Jews, escort him, and heralds proclaim in advance, "Make way before our Lord, the son of David, as is due unto him," the Arabic words being "Amilu tarik la Saidna ben Daud." He is mounted on a horse, and is attired in robes of silk and embroidery with a large turban on his head, and from the turban is suspended a long white cloth adorned with a chain upon which the cipher of Mohammed is engraved. Then he appears before the Caliph and kisses his hand, and the

Caliph rises and places him on a throne which Mohammed had ordered to be made for him, and all the Mohammedan princes who attend the court of the Caliph rise up before him. And the Head of the Captivity is seated on his throne opposite to the Caliph, in compliance with the command of Mohammed to give effect to what is written in the law— "The sceptre shall not depart from Judah nor a law-giver from between his feet, until he come to Shiloh: and to him shall the gathering of the people be." The authority of the Head of the Captivity extends over all the communities of Shinar, Persia, Khurasan and Sheba which is El-Yemen, and Diyar Kalach (Bekr) and the land of Aram Naharaim (Mesopotamia), and over the dwellers in the mountains of Ararat and the land of the Alans[132], which is a land surrounded by mountains and has no outlet except by the iron gates which Alexander made, but which were afterwards broken. Here are the people called Alani. His authority extends also over the land of Siberia, and the communities in the land of the Togarmim unto the mountains of Asveh and the land of Gurgan, the inhabitants of which are called Gurganim who dwell by the river Gihon[133], and these are the Girgashites who follow the Christian religion. Further it extends to the gates of Samarkand, the land of Tibet, and the land of India. In respect of all these countries the Head of the Captivity gives the communities power to appoint Rabbis and Ministers who come unto him to be consecrated and to receive his authority. They bring him offerings and gifts from the ends of the earth. He owns hospices, gardens and plantations in Babylon, and much land inherited from his fathers, and no one can take his possessions from him by force. He has a fixed weekly revenue arising from the hospices of the Jews, the markets and the merchants, apart from that which is brought to him from far-off lands. The man is very rich, and wise in the Scriptures as well as in the Talmud, and many Israelites dine at his table every day.

At his installation, the Head of the Captivity gives much money to the Caliph, to the Princes and the Ministers. On the day that the Caliph performs the ceremony of investing him with authority, he rides in the second of the royal equipages, and is escorted from the palace of the Caliph to his own house with timbrels and fifes. The Exilarch appoints the Chiefs of the Academies by placing his hand upon their heads, thus installing them in their office[134]. The Jews of the city are learned men and very rich.

In Bagdad there are twenty-eight Jewish Synagogues, situated either in the city itself or in Al-Karkh on the other side of the Tigris; for the river divides the metropolis into two parts. The great synagogue of the Head of the Captivity has columns of marble of various colours overlaid with silver and gold, and on these columns are sentences of the Psalms in golden letters. And in front of the ark are about ten steps of marble; on the topmost step are the seats of the Head of the Captivity and of the Princes of the House of David. The city of Bagdad is twenty miles in circumference, situated in a land of palms, gardens and plantations, the like of which is not to be found in the whole land of Shinar. People come thither with merchandise from all lands. Wise men live there, philosophers who know all manner of wisdom, and magicians expert in all manner of witchcraft.

Thence it is two days to Gazigan which is called Resen. It is a large city containing about 5,000 Jews. In the midst of it is the Synagogue of Rabbah[135]—a large one. He is buried close to the Synagogue, and beneath his sepulchre is a cave where twelve of his pupils are buried.

Thence it is a day's journey to Babylon, which is the Babel of old. The ruins thereof are thirty miles in extent[136]. The ruins of the palace of Nebuchadnezzar are still to be seen there, but people are afraid to enter them on account of the serpents and scorpions. Near at hand, within a distance of a mile, there dwell 3,000 Israelites who pray in the Synagogue of the Pavilion of Daniel, which is ancient and was erected by Daniel. It is built of hewn stones and bricks. Between the Synagogue and the Palace of Nebuchadnezzar is the furnace into which were thrown Hananiah, Mishael, and Azariah, and the site of it lies in a valley[137] known unto all.

Thence it is five parasangs to Hillah, where there are 10,000 Israelites and four Synagogues: that of R. Meir, who lies buried before it; the Synagogue of Mar Keshisha, who is buried in front of it; also the Synagogue of Rab Zeiri, the son of Chama, and the Synagogue of R. Mari; the Jews pray there every day.

Thence it is four miles to the Tower of Babel, which the generation whose language was confounded built of the bricks called Agur. The length of its foundation is about two miles, the breadth of the tower is about forty cubits, and the length thereof two hundred cubits. At every ten cubits' distance there are slopes which go round the tower by which one can ascend to the top[138]. One can see from there a view twenty miles in extent, as the land is level. There fell fire from heaven into the midst of the tower which split it to its very depths.

Thence it is half a day to Kaphri, where there are about 200 Jews. Here is the Synagogue of R. Isaac Napcha, who is buried in front of it. Thence it is three parasangs to the Synagogue of Ezekiel, the prophet of blessed memory, which is by the river Euphrates[139]. It is fronted by sixty turrets, and between each turret there is a minor Synagogue, and in the court of the Synagogue is the ark, and at the back of the Synagogue is the sepulchre of Ezekiel. It is surmounted by a large cupola, and it is a very handsome structure. It was built of old by King Jeconiah, king of Judah, and the 35,000 Jews who came with him, when Evil-merodach brought him forth out of prison. This place is by the river Chebar on the one side, and by the river Euphrates on the other, and the names of Jeconiah and those that accompanied him are engraved on the wall: Jeconiah at the top, and Ezekiel at the bottom. This place is held sacred by Israel as a lesser sanctuary unto this day, and people come from a distance to pray there from the time of the New Year until the Day of Atonement. The Israelites have great rejoicings on these occasions. Thither also come the Head of the Captivity, and the Heads of the Academies from Bagdad. Their camp occupies a space of about two miles, and Arab merchants come there as well. A great gathering like a fair takes place, which is called Fera, and they bring forth a scroll of the Law written on parchment by Ezekiel the Prophet, and read from it on the Day of Atonement. A lamp burns day and night over the sepulchre of Ezekiel; the light thereof has been kept burning from the day that he lighted it himself, and they continually renew the wick thereof, and replenish the oil unto the present day. A large house belonging to the sanctuary is filled with books, some of them from the time of the first temple, and some from the time of the second temple, and he who has no sons consecrates his books to its use. The Jews that come thither to pray from the land of Persia and Media bring the money which their countrymen have offered to the Synagogue of Ezekiel the Prophet. The Synagogue owns property, lands and villages, which belonged to King Jeconiah, and when Mohammed came he confirmed all these rights to the Synagogue of Ezekiel[140]. Distinguished Mohammedans also come hither to pray, so great is their love for Ezekiel the Prophet; and they call it Bar (Dar) Melicha (the Dwelling of Beauty). All the Arabs come there to pray[141].

At a distance of about half a mile from the Synagogue are the sepulchres of Hananiah, Mishael, and Azariah, and upon their sepulchres are large cupolas; and even at times of disturbance no man would dare touch the Mohammedan or Jewish servants who attend at the sepulchre of Ezekiel.

Thence it is three miles to the city of Kotsonath, where there are 300 Jews. Here are the sepulchres of Rab Papa, Rab Huna, Joseph Sinai, and Rab Joseph ben Hama; and before each of them is a Synagogue where the Israelites pray every day. Thence it is three parasangs to Ain Siptha, where there is the sepulchre of the prophet Nahum the Elkoshite. Thence it is a day's journey to Kefar Al-Keram, where are the sepulchres of Rab Chisdai, R. Azariah, R. Akiba, and R. Dosa. Thence it is a half-day's journey to a village in the desert, where there are buried R. David and R. Jehuda and Abaji, R. Kurdiah, Rab Sechora, and Rab Ada. Thence it is a day's journey to the river Raga, where there is the sepulchre of

King Zedekiah. Upon it is a large cupola. Thence it is a day's journey to the city of Kufa, where there is the sepulchre of King Jeconiah. Over it is a big structure, and in front thereof is a Synagogue. There are about 7,000 Jews here. At this place is the large mosque of the Mohammedans, for here is buried Ali ben Abu Talib, the son-in-law of Mohammed, and the Mohammedans come hither . . .

Thence it is a day and a half to Sura, which is Mata Mehasya, where the Heads of the Captivity and the Heads of the Academies dwelt at first[142]. Here is the sepulchre of R. Sherira, and of R. Hai his son of blessed memory, also of R. Saadiah Al-Fiumi, and of Rab Samuel the son of Hofni Hacohen, and of Zephaniah the son of Cushi the son of Gedaliah, the prophet, and of the Princes of the House of David, and of the Heads of the Academies who lived there before the destruction of the town.[143]

Thence it is two days to Shafjathib. Here is a Synagogue which the Israelites built from the earth of Jerusalem and its stones, and they called it Shafjathib, which is by Nehardea.[144]

Thence it is a day and a half's journey to El-Anbar, which was Pumbedita in Nehardea.[145] About 3,000 Jews dwell there. The city lies on the river Euphrates. Here is the Synagogue of Rab and Samuel, and their house of study, and in front of it are their graves.

Thence it is five days to Hillah. From this place it is a journey of twenty-one days by way of the deserts to the land of Saba, which is called the land El-Yemen, lying at the side of the land of Shinar which is towards the North.[146]

Here dwell the Jews called Kheibar, the men of Teima. And Teima is their seat of government where R. Hanan the Nasi rules over them. It is a great city, and the extent of their land is sixteen days' journey. It is surrounded by mountains—the mountains of the north. The Jews own many large fortified cities. The yoke of the Gentiles is hnot upon them. They go forth to pillage and to capture booty from distant lands in conjunction with the Arabs, their neighbours and allies. These Arabs dwell in tents, and they make the desert their home. They own no houses, and they go forth to pillage and to capture booty in the land of Shinar and El-Yemen. All the neighbours of these Jews go in fear of them. Among them are husbandmen and owners of cattle; their land is extensive, and they have in their midst learned and wise men. They give the tithe of all they possess unto the scholars who sit in the house of learning, also to poor Israelites and to the recluses, who are the mourners of Zion and Jerusalem, and who do not eat meat nor taste wine, and sit clad in garments of black. They dwell in caves or underground houses, and fast each day with the exception of the Sabbaths and Festivals, and implore mercy of the Holy One, blessed be He, on account of the exile of Israel, praying that He may take pity upon them, and upon all the Jews, the men of Teima, for the sake of His great Name, also upon Tilmas the great city, in which there are about 100,000 Jews[147]. At this place lives Salmon the Nasi, the brother of Hanan the Nasi; and the land belongs to the two brothers, who are of the seed of David, for they have their pedigree in writing. They address many questions unto the Head of the Captivity—their kinsman in Bagdad—and they fast forty days in the year for the Jews that dwell in exile.

There are here about forty large towns and 200 hamlets and villages. The principal city is Tanai, and in all the districts together there are about 300,000 Jews. The city of Tanai is well fortified, and in the midst thereof the people sow and reap. It is fifteen miles in extent. Here is the palace of the Nasi called Salmon. And in Teima dwells Hanan the Nasi, his brother. It is a beautiful city, and contains gardens and plantations. And Tilmas is likewise a great city; it contains about 100,000 Jews. It is well fortified, and is situated between two high mountains. There are wise, discreet, and rich men amongst the inhabitants. From Tilmas to Kheibar it is three days' journey. People say that the men of Kheibar belong to the tribes of Reuben, Gad, and Manasseh, whom Shalmaneser, king of Assyria, led hither into captivity. They have built strongly-fortified cities, and make war upon all other kingdoms. No man can readily reach their territory, because it is a march of eighteen days' journey through the desert, which is altogether uninhabited, so that no one can enter the land.

Kheibar is a very large city with 50,000 Jews[148]. In it are learned men, and great warriors, who wage war with the men of Shinar and of the land of the north, as well as with the bordering tribes of the land of El-Yemen near them, which latter country is on the confines of India[149]. Returning from their land, it is a journey of twenty-five days to the river Virae, which is in the land of El-Yemen, where about 3,000 Jews dwell[150], and amongst them are many a Rabbi and Dayan.

Thence it takes five days to Basra (Bassorah) which lies on the river Tigris. Here there are 10,000 Jews, and among them are scholars and many rich men. Thence it is two days to the river Samara, which is the commencement of the land of Persia. 1,500 Jews live near the sepulchre of Ezra, the priest, who went forth from Jerusalem to King Artaxerxes and died here. In front of his sepulchre is a large synagogue. And at the side thereof the Mohammedans erected a house of prayer out of their great love and veneration for him, and they like the Jews on that account. And the Mohammedans come hither to pray[151]. Thence it is four days to Khuzistan, which is Elam. This province is not inhabited in its entirety, for part of it lies waste. In the midst of its ruins is Shushan (Susa), the capital, the site of the palace of King Ahasuerus. Here are the remains of a large structure of great antiquity. The city contains about 7,000 Jews and fourteen synagogues.

In front of one of the synagogues is the sepulchre of Daniel of blessed memory. The river Tigris divides the city, and the bridge connects the two parts. On the one side where the Jews dwell is the sepulchre of Daniel. Here the market-places used to be, containing great stores of merchandise, by which the Jews became enriched. On the other side of the bridge they were poor, because they had no market-places nor merchants there, only gardens and plantations. And they became jealous, and said "All this prosperity enjoyed by those on the other side is due to the merits of Daniel the prophet who lies buried there." Then the poor people asked those who dwelt on the other side to place the sepulchre of Daniel in their midst, but the others would not comply. So war prevailed between them for many days, and no one went forth or came in on account of the great strife between them. At length both parties growing tired of this state of things took a wise view of the matter, and made a compact, namely, that the coffin of Daniel should be taken for one year to the one side and for another year to the other side. This they did, and both sides became rich. In the course of time Sinjar Shah-ben-Shah, who ruled over the kingdom of Persia and had forty-five kings subject to his authority, came to this place.

He is called Sultan-al-Fars-al-Khabir in Arabic (the mighty Sovereign of Persia), and it is he who ruled from the river Samara unto the city of Samarkand, and unto the river Gozan and the cities of Media and the mountains of Chafton[152]. He ruled also over Tibet, in the forests whereof one finds the animals from which the musk is obtained[153]. The extent of his Empire is a journey of four months. When this great Emperor Sinjar, king of Persia, saw that they took the coffin of Daniel from one side of the river to the other, and that a great multitude of Jews, Mohammedans and Gentiles, and many people from the country were crossing the bridge, he asked the meaning of this proceeding, and they told him these things. He said, "It is not meet to do this ignominy unto Daniel the prophet, but I command you to measure the bridge from both sides, and to take the coffin of Daniel and place it inside another coffin of crystal, so that the wooden coffin be within that of crystal, and to suspend this from the middle of the bridge by a chain of iron; at this spot you must build a synagogue for all comers, so that whoever wishes to pray there, be he Jew or Gentile, may do so." And to this very day the coffin is suspended from the bridge. And the king commanded that out of respect for Daniel no fisherman should catch fish within a mile above or a mile below.[154]

Thence it takes three days to Rudbar where there are about 20,000 Israelites, and among them are learned and rich men. But the Jews live there under great oppression. Thence it is two days to Nihawand, where there are 4,000 Israelites. Thence it is four days to the land of Mulahid. Here live a people who do not profess the Mohammedan religion, but live on high mountains, and worship the Old Man of the land of the Hashishim[155]. And among them there are four communities of Israel who go forth with them in war-time. They are not under the rule of the king of Persia, but reside in the high mountains, and descend from these mountains to pillage and to capture booty, and then return to the mountains, and none can overcome them. There are learned men amongst the Jews of their land. These Jews are under the authority of the Head of the Captivity in Babylon. Thence it is five days to Amadia where there are about 25,000 Israelites[156]. This is the first of those communities that dwell in the mountains of Chafton, where there are more than 100 Jewish communities. Here is the commencement of the land of Media. These Jews belong to the first captivity which King Shalmanezar led away; and they speak the language in which the Targum is written. Amongst them are learned men. The communities reach from the province of Amadia unto the province of Gilan, twenty-five days distant, on the border of the kingdom of Persia. They are under the authority of the king of Persia, and he raises a tribute from them through the hands of his officer, and the tribute which they pay every year by way of poll tax is one gold amir, which is equivalent to one and one-third maravedi. [This tax has to be paid by all males in the land of Islam who are over the age of fifteen.] At this place (Amadia), there arose this day ten years ago, a man named David Alroy of the city of Amadia[157]. He studied under Chisdai the Head of the Captivity, and under the Head of the Academy Gaon Jacob, in the city of Bagdad, and he was well versed in the Law of Israel, in the Halachah, as well as in the Talmud, and in all the wisdom of the Mohammedans, also in secular literature and in the writings of magicians and soothsayers. He conceived the idea of rebelling against the king of Persia, and of collecting the Jews who live in the mountains of Chafton to go forth and to fight against all the nations, and to march and capture Jerusalem. He showed signs by pretended miracles to the Jews, and said, "The Holy

One, blessed be He, sent me to capture Jerusalem and to free you from the yoke of the Gentiles." And the Jews believed in him and called him their Messiah. When the king of Persia heard of it he sent for him to come and speak with him. Alroy went to him without fear, and when he had audience of the king, the latter asked him, "Art thou the king of the Jews?" He answered, "I am." Then the king was wrath, and commanded that he should be seized and placed in the prison of the king, the place where the king's prisoners were bound unto the day of their death, in the city of Tabaristan which is on the large river Gozan. At the end of three days, whilst the king was sitting deliberating with his princes concerning the Jews who had rebelled, David suddenly stood before them. He had escaped from the prison without the knowledge of any man. And when the king saw him, he said to him, "Who brought thee hither, and who has released thee?" "My own wisdom and skill," answered the other; "for I am not afraid of thee, nor of any of thy servants." The king forthwith loudly bade his servants to seize him, but they answered, "We cannot see any man, although our ears hear him." Then the king and all his princes marvelled at his subtlety; but he said to the king "I will go my way"; so he went forth. And the king went after him; and the princes and servants followed their king until they came to the river-side. Then Alroy took off his mantle and spread it on the face of the water to cross thereon. When the servants of the king saw that he crossed the water on his mantle, they pursued him in small boats, wishing to bring him back, but they were unable, and they said, "There is no wizard like this in the whole world." That self-same day he went a journey of ten days to the city of Amadia by the strength of the ineffable Name, and he told the Jews all that had befallen him, and they were astonished at his wisdom.

After that the king of Persia sent word to the Emir Al-Muminin, the Caliph of the Mohammedans at Bagdad, urging him to warn the Head of the Exile, and the Head of the Academy Gaon Jacob, to restrain David Alroy from executing his designs. And he threatened that he would otherwise slay all the Jews in his Empire. Then all the congregations of the land of Persia were in great trouble. And the Head of the Captivity, and the Head of the Academy Gaon Jacob, sent to Alroy, saying, "The time of redemption is not yet arrived; we have not yet seen the signs thereof; for by strength shall no man prevail. Now our mandate is, that thou cease from these designs, or thou shalt surely be excommunicated from all Israel." And they sent unto Zakkai the Nasi in the land of Assur (Mosul) and unto R. Joseph Burhan-al-mulk the astronomer there, bidding them to send on the letter to Alroy, and furthermore they themselves wrote to him to warn him, but he would not accept the warning. Then there arose a king of the name of Sin-ed-din, the king of the Togarmim, and a vassal of the king of Persia, who sent to the father-in-law of David Alroy, and gave him a bribe of 10,000 gold pieces to slay Alroy in secret[158]. So he went to Alroy's house, and slew him whilst he was asleep on his bed. Thus were his plans frustrated. Then the king of Persia went forth against the Jews that lived in the mountain; and they sent to the Head of the Captivity to come to their assistance and to appease the king. He was eventually appeased by a gift of 100 talents of gold, which they gave him, and the land was at peace thereafter[159].

From this mountain it is a journey of twenty days to Hamadan, which is the great city of Media, where there are 30,000 Israelites. In front of a certain synagogue, there are buried Mordecai an Esther[160].

From thence (Hamadan[161]) it takes four days to Tabaristan, which is situated on the river Gozan. Some [four] thousand Jews live there[162]. Thence it is seven days to Ispahan the great city and the royal residence. It is twelve miles in circumference, and about 15,000 Israelites reside there[163]. The Chief Rabbi is Sar Shalom, who has been appointed by the Head of the Captivity to have jurisdiction over all the Rabbis that are in the kingdom of Persia. Four days onward is Shiraz, which is the city of Fars, and 10,000 Jews live there[164]. Thence it is seven days to Ghaznah the great city on the river Gozan, where there are about 80,000 Israelites[165]. It is a city of commercial importance; people of all countries and tongues come thither with their wares. The land is extensive.

Thence it is five days to Samarkand, which is the great city on the confines of Persia. In it live some 50,000 Israelites, and R. Obadiah the Nasi is their appointed head. Among them are wise and very rich men.

Thence it is four days' journey to Tibet, the country in whose forests the musk is found. Thence it takes twenty-eight days to the mountains of Naisabur by the river Gozan. And there are men of Israel in the land of Persia who say that in the mountains of Naisabur four of the tribes of Israel dwell, namely, the tribe of Dan, the tribe of Zebulun, the tribe of Asher, and the tribe of Naphtali, who were included in the first captivity of Shalmaneser, king of Assyria, as it is written (2 Kings xviii. 11): "And he put them in Halah and in Habor by the river of Gozan and in the cities of the Medes[166]."

The extent of their land is twenty days' journey, and they have cities and large villages in the mountains; the river Gozan forms the boundary on the one side. They are not under the rule of the Gentiles, but they have a prince of their own, whose name is R. Joseph Amarkala the Levite. There are scholars among them. And they sow and reap and go forth to war as far as the land of Cush by way of the desert[167].

They are in league with the Kofar-al-Turak, who worship the wind and live in the wilderness, and who do not eat bread, nor drink wine, but live on raw uncooked meat. They have no noses, and in lieu thereof they have two small holes, through which they breathe. They eat animals both clean and unclean, and they are very friendly towards the Israelites. Fifteen years ago they overran the country of Persia with a large army and took the city of Rayy[168]; they smote it with the edge of the sword, took all the spoil thereof, and returned by way of the wilderness. Such an invasion had not been known in the land of Persia for many years. When the king of Persia heard thereof his anger was kindled against them, and he said, "Not in my days nor in the days of my fathers did an army sally forth from this wilderness. Now I will go and cut off their name from the earth." A proclamation was made throughout his Empire, and he assembled all his armies; and he sought a guide who might show him the way to their encampment. And a certain man said that he would show him the way, as he was one of them. And the king promised that he would enrich him if he did so. And the king asked him as to what provisions they would require for the march through the wilderness. And he replied, "Take with you bread and wine for fifteen days, for you will find no sustenance by the way, till you have reached their land." And they did so, and marched through the wilderness for fifteen days, but they found nothing at all. And their food began to give out, so that man and beast were dying of hunger and thirst. Then the king called the guide, and said to him, "Where is your promise to us that you would find our adversaries?" To which the other replied, "I have mistaken the way." And the king was wroth, and commanded that his head should be struck off. And the king further gave orders throughout the camp that every man who had any food should divide it with his neighbour. And they consumed everything they had including their beasts. And after a further thirteen days' march they reached the mountains of Naisabur, where Jews lived. They came there on the Sabbath, and encamped in the gardens and plantations and by the springs of water which are by the side of the river Gozan. Now it was the time of the ripening of the fruit, and they ate and consumed everything. No man came forth to them, but on the mountains they saw cities and many towers.

Then the king commanded two of his servants to go and inquire of the people who lived in the mountains, and to cross the river either in boats or by swimming. So they searched and found a large bridge, on which there were three towers, but the gate of the bridge was locked. And on the other side of the bridge was a great city. Then they shouted in front of the bridge till a man came forth and asked them what they wanted and who they were. But they did not understand him till an interpreter came who understood their language. And when he asked them, they said, "We are the servants of the king of Persia, and we have come to ask who you are, and whom you serve." To which the other replied: "We are Jews; we have no king and no Gentile prince, but a Jewish prince rules over us."

They then questioned him with regard to the infidels, the sons of Ghuz of the Kofar-al-Turak, and he answered: "Truly they are in league with us, and he who seeks to do them harm seeks our harm." Then they went their way, and told the king of Persia, who was much alarmed. And on a certain day the Jews asked him to join combat with them, but he answered: "I am not come to fight you, but the Kofar-al-Turak, my enemy, and if you fight against me I will be avenged on you by killing all the Jews in my Empire; I know that you are stronger than I am in this place, and my army has come out of this great wilderness starving and athirst. Deal kindly with me and do not fight against me, but leave me to engage with the Kofar-al-Turak, my enemy, and sell me also the provisions which I require for myself and my army." The Jews then took counsel together, and resolved to propitiate the king on account of the Jews who were in exile in his Empire. Then the king entered their land with his army, and stayed there fifteen days. And they showed him much honour, and also sent a dispatch to the Kofar-al-Turak their allies, reporting the matter to them. Thereupon the latter occupied the mountain passes in force with a large army composed of all those who dwelt in that desert, and when the king of Persia went forth to fight with them, they placed themselves in battle array against him. The Kofar-al-Turak army was victorious and slew many of the Persian host, and the king of Persia fled with only a few followers to his own country[169].

Now a horseman, one of the servants of the king of Persia, enticed a Jew, whose name was R. Moses, to come with him, and when he came to the land of Persia this horseman made the Jew his slave. One day the archers came before the king to give a display of their skill and no one among them could be found to draw the bow like this R. Moses. Then the king inquired of him by means of an interpreter who knew his language, and he related all that the horseman had done to him. Thereupon the king at once granted him his liberty, had him clad in robes of silk, gave him gifts, and said to him, "If thou wilt embrace our religion, I will make thee a rich man and steward of my house," but he answered, My lord,

I cannot do this thing." Then the king took him and placed him in the house of the Chief Rabbi of the Ispahan community, Sar Shalom, who gave him his daughter to wife. This same R. Moses told me all these things.

Thence one returns to the land of Khuzistan which is by the river Tigris, and one goes down the river which falls into the Indian Ocean unto an island called Kish[170]. It is a six days' journey to reach this island. The inhabitants neither sow nor reap. They possess only one well, and there is no stream in the whole island, but they drink rain-water. The merchants who come from India and the islands encamp there with their wares. Moreover, men from Shinar, El-Yemen and Persia bring thither all sorts of silk, purple and flax, cotton, hemp, worked wool, wheat, barley, millet, rye, and all sorts of food, and lentils of every description, and they trade with one another, whilst the men from India bring great quantities of spices thither. The islanders act as middlemen, and earn their livelihood thereby. There are about 500 Jews there.

Thence it is ten days' journey by sea to Katifa, where there are about 5,000 Jews. Here the bdellium is to be found[171]. On the twenty-fourth of Nisan rain falls upon the water, upon the surface of which certain small sea-animals float which drink in the rain and then shut themselves up, and sink to the bottom. And about the middle of Tishri men descend to the bed of the sea by ropes, and collect these shell-fish, then split them open and extract the pearls. This pearl-fishery belongs to the King of the country, but is controlled by a Jewish official.

Thence it is seven days' journey to Khulam which is the beginning of the country of the Sun-worshippers[172]. These are the sons of Cush, who read the stars, and are all black in colour. They are honest in commerce. When merchants come to them from distant lands and enter the harbour, three of the King's secretaries go down to them and record their names, and then bring them before the King, whereupon the King makes himself responsible even for their property which they leave in the open, unprotected. There is an official who sits in his office, and the owner of any lost property has only to describe it to him when he hands it back. This custom prevails in all that country. From Passover to New Year, that is all during the summer, no man can go out of his house because of the sun, for the heat in that country is intense, and from the third hour of the day onward, everybody remains in his house till the evening. Then they go forth and kindle lights in all the market places and all the streets, and then do their work and business at night-time. For they have to turn night into day in consequence of the great heat of the sun. Pepper is found there. They plant the trees thereof in the fields, and each man of the city knows his own plantation. The trees are small, and the pepper is as white as snow. And when they have collected it, they place it in saucepans and pour boiling water over it, so that it may become strong. They then take it out of the water and dry it in the sun, and it turns black. Calamus and ginger and many other kinds of spice are found in this land.

The people of this country do not bury their dead, but embalm them by means of various spices, after which they place them on chairs and cover them with fine linen. And each family has a house where it preserves the embalmed remains of its ancestors and relations. The flesh hardens on the bones, and the embalmed bodies look like living beings, so that every man can recognize his parents, and the members of his family for many years. They worship the sun, and they have high places everywhere outside the city at a distance of p. 92 about half a mile. And every morning they run forth to greet the sun, for on every high place a solar disc is made of cunning workmanship and as the sun rises the disc rotates with thundering noise, and all, both men and women, offer incense to the sun with censers in their hands. Such are their superstitious practices. And throughout the island, including all the towns there, live several thousand Israelites. The inhabitants are all black, and the Jews also. The latter are good and benevolent. They know the law of Moses and the prophets, and to a small extent the Talmud and Halacha.

Thence it is twenty-three days by sea to Ibrig[173], and the inhabitants are fire-worshippers, and are called Duchbin. Among them are about

3,000 Jews, and these Duchbin have priests in their several temples who are great wizards in all manner of witchcraft, and there are none like them in all the earth. In front of the high place of their temple there is a deep trench, where they keep a great fire alight all the year, and they call it Elahutha. And they cause their sons and daughters to pass through the fire, and even their dead they throw into it. Some of the great men of the country make a vow to die by fire. In such cases the man communicates his intention to the members of his household and his relations, and says:—"I have vowed to throw myself in the fire whilst I am yet alive," then they answer, saying: "Happy art thou." And when the day of the performance of his vow arrives, they prepare for him a grand banquet, and if he is rich he rides on horseback, if poor he goes on foot to the border of the trench and throws himself into the fire. And all the members of his family shout to the accompaniment of timbrels and dancing until the body is entirely consumed. At the end of three days two of their high priests come to his house and to his children and say unto them: "Arrange the house, for this day your father will come to give his last directions as to what ye shall do." And they bring witnesses from the city. Then Satan is made to appear in the likeness of the deceased, and when his widow and children ask him how he fares in the other world he answers: "I went to my companions, but they would not receive me until I had discharged my obligations to the members of my house and to my neighbours." Then he makes his will and divides his property among his children, and gives directions that all his creditors should be paid and that his debts should be collected. Then the witnesses write out the will, and he goes his way and is seen no more. And by means of this trickery and witchcraft which these priests practise, the people are confirmed in their errors and assert that there is none in all the land like their priests.

Thence to cross over to the land of Zin (China) is a voyage of forty days. Zin is in the uttermost East, and some say that there is the Sea of Nikpa (Ning-po?), where the star Orion predominates and stormy winds prevail[174]. At times the helmsman cannot govern his ship, as a fierce wind drives her into this Sea of Nikpa, where she cannot move from her place; and the crew have to remain where they are till their stores of food are exhausted and then they die. In this way many a ship has been lost, but men eventually discovered a device by which to escape from this evil place. The crew provide themselves with hides of oxen. And when this evil wind blows which drives them into the Sea of Nikpa, they wrap themselves up in the skins, which they make waterproof, and, armed with knives, plunge into the sea. A great bird called the griffin spies them out, and in the belief that the sailor is an animal, the griffin seizes hold of him, brings him to dry land, and puts him down on a mountain or in a hollow in order to devour him. The man then quickly thrusts at the bird with a knife and slays him. Then the man issues forth from the skin and walks till he comes to an inhabited place. And in this manner many a man escapes[175].

Thence to Al-Gingaleh is a voyage of fifteen days, and about 1,000 Israelites dwell there. Thence by sea to Chulan is seven days; but no Jews live there. From there it is twelve days to Zebid, where there are a few Jews. From there it is eight days' journey to India which is on the mainland, called the land of Aden, and this is the Eden which is in Thelasar[176]. The country is mountainous. There are many Israelites here, and they are not under the yoke of the Gentiles, but possess cities and castles on the summits of the mountains, from which they make descents into the plain-country called Lybia, which is a Christian Empire. These are the Lybians of the land of Lybia, with whom the Jews are at war. The Jews take spoil and booty and retreat to the mountains, and no man can prevail against them. Many of these Jews of the land of Aden come to Persia and Egypt[177].

Thence to the land of Assuan is a journey of twenty days through the desert. This is Seba on the river Pishon (Nile) which descends from the land of Cush[178]. And some of these sons of Cush have a king whom they call the Sultan Al-Habash. There is a people among them who, like animals, eat of the herbs that grow on the banks of the Nile and in the fields. They go about naked and have not the intelligence of ordinary men. They cohabit with their sisters and any one they find. The climate is very hot. When the men of Assuan make a raid into their land, they take with them bread and wheat, dry grapes and figs, and throw the food to these people, who run after it. Thus they bring many of them back prisoners, and sell them in the land of Egypt and in the surrounding countries. And these are the black slaves, the sons of Ham.

From Assuan it is a distance of twelve days to Heluan where there are about 300 Jews. Thence people travel in caravans a journey of fifty days through the great desert called Sahara, to the land of Zawilah, which is Havilah in the land of Gana[179]. In this desert there are mountains of sand, and when the wind rises, it covers the caravans with the sand, and many die from suffocation. Those that escape bring back with them copper, wheat, fruit, all manner of lentils, and salt. And from thence they bring gold, and all kinds of jewels. This is in the land of Cush which is called Al-Habash on the western confines[180]. From Heluan it is thirteen days' journey to Kutz which is Kûs, and this is the commencement of the land of Egypt. At Kutz there are 300 Jews[181]. Thence it is 300 miles to Fayum, which is Pithom, where there are 200 Jews; and unto this very day one can see ruins of the buildings which our forefathers erected there[182].

Thence to Mizraim is a journey of four days. This Mizraim is the great city situated on the banks of the Nile, which is Pison or Al-Nil[183]. The number of Jewish inhabitants is about 7,000. Two large synagogues are there, one belonging to the men of the land of Israel and one belonging to the men of the land of Babylon. The synagogue of the men of the land of Israel is called Kenisat-al-Schamiyyin, and the synagogue of the men of Babylon is called Kenisat-al-Irakiyyin. Their usage with regard to the portions and sections of the Law is not alike; for the men of Babylon are accustomed to read a portion every week, as is done in Spain, and is our custom, and to finish the Law each year; whilst the men of Palestine do not do so, but divide each portion into three sections and finish the Law at the end of three years. The two communities, however, have an established custom to unite and pray together on the day of the Rejoicing of the Law, and on the day of the Giving of the Law[184]. Among the Jews is Nethanel the Prince of

Princes and the head of the Academy, who is the head of all the congregations in Egypt[185]; he appoints Rabbis and officials, and is attached to the court of the great King, who lives in his palace of Zoan el-Medina, which is the royal city for the Arabs. Here resides the Emir al Muminin, a descendant of Abu Talib. All his subjects are called "Alawiyyim[186]," because they rose up against the Emir al Muminin al Abbasi (the Abbaside Caliph) who resides at Bagdad. And between the two parties there is a lasting feud, for the former have set up a rival throne in Zoan (Egypt).

Twice in the year the Egyptian monarch goes forth, once on the occasion of the great festival, and again when the river Nile rises. Zoan is surrounded by a wall, but Mizraim has no wall, for the river encompasses it on one side. It is a great city, and it has market-places as well as inns in great number. The Jews that dwell there are very rich. No rain falls, neither is ice or snow ever seen. The climate is very hot.

The river Nile rises once a year in the month of Elul; it covers all the land, and irrigates it to a distance of fifteen days' journey. The waters remain upon the surface of the land during the months of Elul and Tishri, and irrigate and fertilize it.

The inhabitants have a pillar of marble, erected with much skill, in order to ascertain the extent of the rise of the Nile. It stands in the front of an island in the midst of the water, and is twelve cubits high[187]. When the Nile rises and covers the column, they know that the river has risen and has covered the land for a distance of fifteen days' journey to its full extent. If only half the column is covered, the water only covers half the extent of the land. And day by day an officer takes a measurement on the column and makes proclamation thereof in Zoan and in the city of Mizraim, proclaiming: "Give praise unto the Creator, for the river this day has risen to such and such a height"; each day he takes the measurement and makes his proclamation. If the water covers the entire column, there will be abundance throughout Egypt. The river continues to rise gradually till it covers the land to the extent of fifteen days' journey. He who owns a field hires workmen, who dig deep trenches in his field, and fish come with the rise of the water and enter the trenches. Then, when the waters have receded, the fish remain behind in the trenches, and the owners of the fields take them and either eat them or sell them to the fishmongers, who salt them and deal in them in every place. These fish are exceedingly fat and large, and the oil obtained from them is used in this land for lamp-oil. Though a man eat a great quantity of these fish, if he but drink Nile water afterwards they will not hurt him, for the waters have medicinal properties.

People ask, what causes the Nile to rise? The Egyptians say that up the river, in the land of Al-Habash (Abyssinia), which is the land of Havilah, much rain descends at the time of the rising of the river, and that this abundance of rain causes the river to rise and to cover the surface of the land[188]. If the river does not rise, there is no sowing, and famine is sore in the land. Sowing is done in the month of Marheshwan, after the river has gone back to its ordinary channel. In the month of Adar is the barley-harvest, and in the month of Nisan the wheat-harvest.

In the month of Nisan they have cherries, pears, cucumbers, and gourds in plenty, also beans, peas, chickpeas, and many kinds of vegetables, such as purslane, asparagus, pulse, lettuce, coriander, endive, cabbage, leek, and cardoon. The land is full of all good things, and the gardens and plantations are watered from the various reservoirs and by the river-water.

The river Nile, after flowing past (the city of) Mizraim, divides into four heads: one channel proceeds in the direction of Damietta, which is Caphtor[189], where it falls into the sea. The second channel flows to the city of Reshid (Rosetta), which is near Alexandria, and there falls into the sea; the third channel goes by way of Ashmun, where it falls into the sea; and the fourth channel goes as far as the frontier of Egypt[190]. Along both banks of these four river-heads are cities, towns and villages, and people visit these places either by ship or by land. There is no such thickly-populated land as this elsewhere. It is extensive too and abundant in all good things.

From New Mizraim unto Old Mizraim is a distance of two parasangs. The latter is in ruins, and the place where walls and houses stood can be seen to the present day. The store-houses also of Joseph of blessed memory are to be found in great numbers in many places. They are built of lime and stone, and are exceedingly strong[191]. A pillar is there of marvellous workmanship, the like of which cannot be seen throughout the world.

Outside the city is the ancient synagogue of Moses our master, of blessed memory, and the overseer and clerk of this place of worship is a venerable old man; he is a man of learning, and they call him Al Sheik Abu al-Nazr[192]. The extent of Mizraim, which is in ruins, is three miles. Thence to the land of Goshen is eight parasangs; here is Bilbais[193]. There are about 300 Jews in the city, which is a large one. Thence it is half a day's journey to Ain-al-Shams or Ramses, which is in ruins. Traces are there to be seen of the buildings which our fore-fathers raised, namely, towers built of bricks. From here it is a day's journey to Al Bubizig, where there are about 200 Jews. Thence it is half a day to Benha, where there are about 60 Jews. Thence it takes half a day to Muneh Sifte, where there are 500 Jews[194]. From there it is half a day's journey to Samnu, where there are about 200 Jews. Thence it is four parasangs to Damira, where there are about 700 Jews. From there it is five days to Lammanah, where there are about 500 Jews[195]. Two days' journey takes one to Alexandria of Egypt, which is Ammon of No; but when Alexander of Macedon built the city, he called it after his own name, and made it exceedingly strong and beautiful[196]. The houses, the palaces, and the walls are of excellent architecture. Outside the town is the academy of Aristotle, the teacher of Alexander. This is a large building, standing between other academies to the number of twenty, with a column of marble between each. People from the whole world were wont to come hither in order to study the wisdom of Aristotle the philosopher. The city is built over a hollow by means of arches. Alexander built it with great understanding. The streets are wide and straight, so that a man can look along them for a mile from gate to gate, from the gate of Reshid to the gate by the sea.

Alexander also built for the harbour of Alexandria a pier, a king's highway running into the midst of the sea. And there he erected a large tower, a lighthouse, called Manar al Iskandriyyah in Arabic. On the top of the tower there is a glass mirror. Any ships that attempted to attack or molest the city, coming from Greece or from the Western lands, could be seen by means of this mirror of glass at a distance of twenty days' journey, and the inhabitants could thereupon put themselves on their guard. It happened once, many years after the death of Alexander, that a ship came from the land of Greece, and the name of the captain was Theodoros, a Greek of great cleverness. The Greeks at that time were under the yoke of Egypt. The captain brought great gifts in silver and gold and garments of silk to the King of Egypt, and he moored his ship in front of the lighthouse, as was the custom of all merchants.

Every day the guardian of the lighthouse and his servants had their meals with him, until the captain came to be on such friendly terms with the keeper that he could go in and out at all times. And one day he gave a banquet, and caused the keeper and all his servants to drink a great deal of wine. When they were all asleep, the captain and his servants arose and broke the mirror and departed that very night. From that day onward the Christians began to come thither with boats and large ships, and eventually captured the large island called Crete and also Cyprus, which are under the dominion of the Greeks. [The other MSS. add here: Ever since then, the men of the King of Egypt have been unable to prevail over the Greeks.] To this day the lighthouse is a landmark to all seafarers who come to Alexandria; for one can see it at a distance of 100 miles by day, and at night the keeper lights a torch which the mariners can see from a distance, and thus sail towards it[197].

Alexandria is a commercial market for all nations. Merchants come thither from all the Christian kingdoms: on the one side, from the land of Venetia and Lombardy, Tuscany, Apulia, Amalfi, Sicilia, Calabria, Romagna, Khazaria, Patzinakia, Hungaria, Bulgaria, Rakuvia (Ragusa?), Croatia, Slavonia, Russia, Alamannia (Germany), Saxony, Danemark, Kurland? Ireland? Norway (Norge?), Frisia, Scotia, Angleterre, Wales, Flanders, Hainault? Normandy, France, Poitiers, Anjou, Burgundy, Maurienne, Provence, Genoa, Pisa, Gascony, Aragon, and Navarra[198], and towards the west under the sway of the Mohammedans, Andalusia, Algarve, Africa and the land of the Arabs: and on the other side India, Zawilah, Abyssinia, Lybia, El-Yemen, Shinar, Esh-Sham (Syria); also Javan, whose people are called the Greeks, and the Turks. And merchants of India bring thither all kinds of spices, and the merchants of Edom buy of them. And the city is a busy one and full of traffic. Each nation has an inn of its own.

By the sea-coast there is a sepulchre of marble on which are engraved all manner of beasts and birds; an effigy is in the midst thereof, and all the writing is in ancient characters, which no one knows now. Men suppose that it is the sepulchre of a king who lived in early times before the Deluge. The length of the sepulchre is fifteen spans, and its breadth is six spans. There are about 3,000 Jews in Alexandria.

Thence it is two days' journey to Damietta which is Caphtor, where there are about 200 Jews, and it lies upon the sea. Thence it is one day's journey to Simasim; it contains about 100 Jews. From there it is half a day to Sunbat; the inhabitants sow flax and weave linen, which they export to all parts of the world[199]. Thence it is four days to Ailam, which is Elim[200]. It belongs to the Arabs who dwell in the wilderness. Thence it is two days' journey to Rephidim where the Arabs dwell, but there are no Jews there[201]. A day's journey from thence takes one to Mount Sinai. On the top of the mountain is a large convent belonging to the great monks called Syrians[202]. At the foot of the mountain is a large town called Tur Sinai; the inhabitants speak the language of the Targum (Syriac). It is close to a small mountain, five days distant from Egypt. The inhabitants are under Egyptian rule. At a day's journey from Mount Sinai is [[203]the Red Sea, which is an arm of the Indian Ocean. We return to Damietta. From there it is a day's journey to] Tanis, which is Hanes, where there are about 40 Jews. It is an island in the midst of the sea[204]. Thus far extends the empire of Egypt.

Thence it takes twenty days by sea to Messina, which is the commencement of Sicily and is situated on the arm of the sea that is called Lipar[205], which divides it from Calabria. Here about 200 Jews dwell. It is a land full of everything good, with gardens and plantations. Here most of the pilgrims assemble to cross over to Jerusalem, as this is the best crossing. Thence it is about two days' journey to Palermo, which is a large city. Here is the palace of King William. Palermo contains about 1,500 Jews and a large number of Christians and Mohammedans[206]. It is in a district abounding in springs and brooks of water, a land of wheat and barley, likewise of gardens and plantations, and there is not the like thereof in the whole island of Sicily. Here is the domain and garden of the king, which is called Al Harbina (Al Hacina)[207], containing all sorts of fruit-trees. And in it is a large fountain. The garden is encompassed by a wall. And a reservoir has been made there which is called Al Buheira[208], and in it are many sorts of fish. Ships overlaid with silver and gold are there, belonging to the king, who takes pleasure-trips in them with his women[209]. In the park there is also a great palace, the walls of which are painted, and overlaid with gold and silver; the paving of the floors is of marble, picked out in gold and silver in all manner of designs. There is no building like this anywhere. And this island, the commencement of which is Messina, contains all the pleasant things of this world. It embraces Syracuse, Marsala, Catania, Petralia, and Trapani, the circumference of the island being six days' journey. In Trapani coral is found, which is called Al Murgan[210].

Thence people pass to the city of Rome in ten days. And from Rome they proceed by land to Lucca, which is a five days' journey. Thence they cross the mountain of Jean de Maurienne, and the passes of Italy. It is twenty days' journey to Verdun, which is the commencement of Alamannia, a land of mountains and hills. All the congregations of Alamannia are situated on the great river Rhine, from the city of Cologne, which is the principal town of the Empire, to the city of Regensburg, a distance of fifteen days' journey at the other extremity of Alamannia, otherwise called Ashkenaz. And the following are the cities in the land of Alamannia, which have Hebrew congregations: Metz, Treves on the river Moselle, Coblenz, Andernach, Bonn, Cologne, Bingen, Münster, Worms,[211] [All Israel is dispersed in every land, and he who does not further the gathering of Israel will not meet with happiness nor live with Israel. When the Lord will remember us in our exile, and raise the horn of his anointed, then every one will say, "I will lead the Jews and I will gather them." As for the towns which have been mentioned, they contain scholars and communities that love their brethren, and speak peace to those that are near and afar, and when a wayfarer comes they rejoice, and make a feast for him, and say, "Rejoice, brethren, for the help of the Lord comes in the twinkling of an eye." If we were not afraid that the appointed time has not yet arrived nor been reached, we would have gathered together, but we dare not do so until the time for song has arrived, and the voice of the turtle-dove (is heard in the land), when the messengers will come and say continually, "The Lord be exalted." Meanwhile they send missives one to the other, saying, "Be ye strong in the law of Moses, and do ye mourners for Zion and ye mourners for Jerusalem entreat the Lord, and may the supplication of those that wear the garments of mourning be received through their merits." In addition to the several cities which we have mentioned there are besides] Strassburg, Würzburg, Mantern, Bamberg, Freising, and Regensburg at the extremity of the Empire[212]. In these cities there are many Israelites, wise men and rich.

Thence extends the land of Bohemia, called Prague[213]. This is the commencement of the land of Slavonia, and the Jews who dwell there call it Canaan, because the men of that land (the Slavs) sell their sons and their daughters to the other nations. These are the men of Russia, which is a great empire stretching from the gate of Prague to the gates of Kieff, the large city which is at the extremity of that empire[214]. It is a land of mountains and forests, where there are to be found the animals called vair[215], ermine, and sable. No one issues forth from his house in winter-time on account of the cold. People are to be found there who have lost the tips of their noses by reason of the frost. Thus far reaches the empire of Russia.

The kingdom of France, which is Zarfath, extends from the town of Auxerre[216] unto Paris, the great city—a journey of six days. The city belongs to King Louis. It is situated on the river Seine. Scholars are there, unequalled in the whole world, who study the Law day and night. They are charitable and hospitable to all travellers, and are as brothers and friends unto all their brethren the Jews. May God, the Blessed One, have mercy upon us and upon them!

Finished and completed.

\* \* \* \* \*

# FOOTNOTES:

\* \* \* \* \*

1 Tudela was called in Benjamin's time *Tuteila*. Sepharad is Spain.
2 There is a considerable difference of opinion as to the exact dates at which Benjamin began and completed his journey. In my opinion, the period can be placed within a very narrow compass. Early in his journey he visited Rome, where he found R. Jechiel to be the steward of the household of Pope Alexander. This can be no other than Pope Alexander III, who played so important a part in the struggle between King Henry II and Thomas a Becket. The German Emperor, Frederick Barbarossa, supported the anti-Pope Victor IV, and in consequence Alexander had to leave Rome soon after his election in 1159 and before his consecration. He did not return to settle down permanently in Rome until November 23, 1165, but was forced to leave again in 1167. Consequently Benjamin must have been in Rome between the end of 1165 and 1167. Benjamin terminated his travels by passing from Egypt to Sicily and Italy, then crossing the Alps and visiting Germany. In Cairo he found that the Fatimite Caliph was the acknowledged ruler. The Caliph here referred to must have been El-'Adid, who died on Monday, September 13, 1171—being the last of the Fatimite line. A short time before his death, Saladin had become the virtual ruler of Egypt, and had ordered the Khotba to be read in the name of the Abbaside Caliph el-Mostadi of Bagdad. (See

the *Life of Saladin*, by Bohadin: Palestine Pilgrims' Text Society, p. 61.) It is clear, therefore, that Benjamin's absence from Europe must be placed between the years 1166 and 1171. Benjamin on his return journey passed through Sicily when the island was no longer governed by a viceroy. King William II (the Good) attained his majority in 1169, and Benjamin's visit took place subsequently. It will be found in the course of the narrative that not a single statement by Benjamin is inconsistent with this determination of date; see p. 3, n. 4; p. 9, n. 2; p. 15, n. 4; p. 61, n. 1; and p. 79, n. 2.

3 Saragossa was called in Benjamin's time *Sarakosta* (= Caesar-Augusta). Charisi, in *Tachkemoni*, 46, refers to some of the Rabbis.

4 The imposing ruins at Tarragona comprise prehistoric walls of enormous unhewn blocks of stone, as well as the remains of Roman aqueducts, tombs, amphitheatres, &c. Here and generally in this narrative the letter R is used as an abbreviation for Rabbi.

5 See Graetz, *Geschichte der Juden*, vol. VI, pp. 230 et seq.; also notes 1 and 10 at the end of vol. VI.

6 The ancient name of Gerona was Gerunda.

7 See Geiger's *Jüdische Zeitschrift für Wissenschaft und Leben*, p. 281. The Records of Narbonne bear evidence of sales of lands standing in the name of R. Kalonymos (*Archives Israelites*, 1861, p. 449). His ancestor, R. Machir, came to Europe in the time of Charlemagne.

8 R. Abraham ben Isaac (Rabad II) was author of the Rabbinic code; Ha-Eshkol, and was one of the intermediaries between the Talmudists of France and the Scholars of Spain. He died 1178.

9 A parasang is about 3-2/5 English miles, and the distance from Narbonne to Beziers is correctly given. 10 parasangs make a day's journey.

10 The King of Portugal is even now styled King of the Algarves.

11  Cf. Graetz, VI, p. 240, also Joseph Jacob's *Angevin Jews*, p. 111. R. Asher was one of a group of pious Rabbis known as Perushim—who might be styled Jewish monks. His father, Rabbenu Meshullam, died 1170.

12  He is referred to in *Tosafoth Temurah*, fol. 12a and b.

13  This eminent Talmudist, known as the Rabad, was son-in-law of the R. Abraham of Narbonne before referred to. See Graetz, VI, 243.

14  The Abbey of St. Aegidius was much resorted to in the Middle Ages. The Jews of Beaucaire, and the neighbourhood, enjoyed the patronage of Raymond V, Count of Toulouse, called by the Troubadour poets "the good Duke." See Graetz, VI, note I, p. 401. It is impossible to enlarge in these notes upon the several Jewish scholars referred to by Benjamin. An interesting article by Professor Israel Levi on the "Jews in Mediaeval France," and other articles, in the *Jewish Encyclopaedia*, also Gross, *Gallia Judaica*, might be consulted with advantage.

15  The BM. MS. calls R. Abba Mari dead, which statement, unless qualified, as in a few other instances, by the insertion of the word "since," would be unintelligible.

16  Asher's Text and Epstein's MS. give the distance between Arles and Marseilles as three days' journey. The actual distance is about fifty-three English miles. Probably the Roman roads were still in use.

17  R. Isaac, son of Abba Mari, is the celebrated author of "Baal Haittur"; he wrote this work at Marseilles, 1179. It is doubtful whether he was the son of Count Raymond's bailiff.

18  His full name is R. Jacob Perpignano. See Graetz, VI, note 1, p. 399.

19  The meaning of course is that the Genoese pillage Christian and Mohammedan places alike.

20  See Dr. H. Berliner's work *Die Geschichte der Juden in Rom*. His derivation of the Hebrew word used for Pope, אפיפיור from Peter, is questionable. It is the Greek ἐπίφορος. See Talmud, *Aboda Zarah*, 11 a.

21  The great work alluded to is the *Talmudical Dictionary*, completed in 1101. See Graetz, VI, p. 281.

22  The palace of the Caesars on the Palatine Hill is no doubt here referred to.

23  בהורה, quoted by E and Asher, is a corrupt reading for בתוכה.

24  This is Josippon's story. Benjamin occasionally embodies in his work fantastic legends told him, or recorded by his predecessors. His authorities lived in the darkest period of the Middle Ages. Josippon, Book I, Chap, iv, speaks of 320 senators. I have followed Breithaupt, and rendered יושיש "consul."

25  Having regard to the various readings, it is possible that the Thermae of Diocletian or more probably the Flavian amphitheatre, which early in the Middle Ages began to be called the Colosseum, is here referred to. It had four stories, each floor composed of arcades containing eighty separate compartments, making 320 in all. Our author in the course of his narrative speaks more than once of buildings erected on a uniform plan corresponding with the days of the year.

26  I. Heilprin, the author of *Seder Hadoroth* (Warsaw, 1897 edition, p. 157) as well as Zunz, appear to have here fallen into error, assuming as they do that Benjamin refers to the ten teachers of the Mishna, R. Gamaliel, R. Akiba and the other sages who suffered martyrdom in Palestine at the hands of the Roman Emperors. The ten martyrs here alluded to are those referred to in the Preface to Hakemoni, published by Geiger in

תדרגו מלא ופנים, Berlin, 1840, and ספר הטירים, Berlin edition, fols. 151-2
עשרה צדיקים ורבנים וחכמים ז"ל ר' חזקיה ור' הגנאל הגדול והצדיק נ"ע קרובינו קרוב לוקחי
ר' יואל, ר' אמנון, ור' אוריאל הר' הצדיק ז"ל ור' מנחם ור' חייא ור' משה ור' דוד ור'
צדק ור' ירמיה ור' אוריאל וקנים הטירים ראטי הקהל ומניניני העיר ורבנים ז"ל לחיי הצ"ה
אמן. Rome, as so many other cities, had its own martyrs.

27  This is the statue of Marcus Aurelius now before the Capitol.
28  Even in Benjamin's time the Campagna was noted for malaria.
29  Professor Ray Lankester, in a lecture given on Dec. 29, 1903, at the Royal Institution, illustrated changes in the disposition of land and water by pointing to the identical ruined Temple referred to by Benjamin. It now stands high above the sea, and did so in the second and third centuries of the present era, but in the eighth and ninth centuries was so low, owing to the sinking of the land, that the lower parts of its marble pillars stood in the sea, and sea-shells grew in the crevices.
30  Josippon gives these legends in Book I, chaps. iii and iv, when speaking of Zur, whom he associates with Sorrento. Benjamin had few other sources of information. In the immediate neighbourhood of Pozzuoli is Solfatara, where sulphur is found. A destructive eruption from the crater took place in 1198. Hot springs abound, and the baths at Bagnoli are much frequented to the present day. The underground road is the Piedi grotta of Posilipo, constructed by Augustus.
31  R. Isaac, the father of R. Judah, must be the "Greek Locust" against whom Ibn Ezra directed his satire when visiting Salerno some twenty years before R. Benjamin. See Graetz, VI, p. 441.
32  Cf. Isaiah lxvi. 19.
33  This city was destroyed by William the Bad in 1156. It was ordered to be restored by William the Good in 1169, so that Benjamin must have visited Bari before that date. See p. 79, note 2. We have here another clue as to the date of Benjamin's travels.

34     See H. M. Adler's article on Jews in Southern Italy, *J.Q.R.*, XIV, p. 111. Gibbon, *Decline and Fall of the Roman Empire*, chap. lvi, describing the reconquest of the southern provinces of Italy by the Byzantine Emperor Manuel, 1155, says. "The natives of Calabria were still attached to the Greek language and worship."

35     The river Achelous falls into the Ionian Sea opposite to Ithaca.

36     Anatolica is now known as Aetolicum.

37     Patras, the ancient Patrae, was founded long before the time of Antipater. *Josippon*, II, chap. xxiii, is again the questionable authority on which Benjamin relied.

38     Lepanto in the early Middle Ages was called Naupactus or Epacto, and to reach it from Patras the Gulf of Corinth had to be crossed.

39     Chalcis, the capital of Euboea or Negroponte, is even now called Egripo. It is situated on the Straits of Euripus.

40     Some twenty years later the Wallachians were in open revolt and became independent of the Byzantine Empire. Gibbon, chap. lx.

41     See Gibbon, chap. liii. He often quotes Benjamin.

42     The Grand Duchy of Kieff was called Russia. See page 81.

43     The Petchinegs, as well as the Khazars, Bulgarians, Hungarians, and Turks, are called by Josippon, I, chap. i, descendants of Togarma. Patzinakia was the country from the Danube to the Dnieper, and corresponds with Dacia of classical times.

44     The readings of E and A are corrupt. R has נוריאה, and BM. has נורית, the southern provinces of Russia were spoken of as the land of the Khazars, especially by Jewish writers, long after the Russian conquest about the year 1000, and the Crimea was known to European travellers as Gazaria. It took Rabbi Pethachia eight days to pass through the land of the Khazars. See Dr. A. Benisch, *Translation of Petachia's Travels*. In note 3, p. 70, he gives a

short sketch of their history. The ruling dynasty and most of the inhabitants embraced the Jewish religion.

45 *Procopius*, vol. I (Palestine Pilgrims' Text Society), gives a full description of Constantinople.

46 The commentator, wrongly supposed to be Rashi, gives an interesting note upon the passage in I Chron. xx. 2, where it is mentioned that David took the crown of the king of the children of Ammon, and found it to weigh a talent of gold, and it was set upon David's head. Rashi states that the meaning of the passage must be that this crown was hung above David's throne, and adds that he heard in Narbonne that this practice was still kept up by the kings in the East.

47 See for a full account of these powerful Seljuk Sultans F. Lebrecht's Essay on the Caliphate of Bagdad during the latter half of the twelfth century. Vol. II of A. Asher's *Itinerary of Rabbi Benjamin.*

48 Ibn Verga, *Shevet Jehuda*, XXV, states that a predecessor of the Emperor Manuel Comnenus issued an edict prohibiting the Jews from residing elsewhere than in Pera, and restricting their occupation to tanning and shipbuilding.

49 This place is mentioned by *Procopius*, p. 119, as having been fortified by Justinian. It is now known as Rodosto.

50 Ibn Ezra visited Cyprus before his arrival in London in 1158, when he wrote the *Sabbath Epistle*. It is not unlikely that the heterodox practices of the sect of whom Benjamin here speaks had been put forward in certain books to which Ibn Ezra alludes, and induced him to compose the pamphlet in defence of the traditional mode of observance of the Sabbath day. This supposition is not inconsistent with Graetz's theory, vol. VI, p. 447. See also Dr. Friedlander, *Ibn Ezra in England, J.Q.R.*, VIII, p. 140, and Joseph Jacobs, *The Jews of Angevin England*, p. 35.

51 See Gibbon, chaps, lviii and lix; Charles Mills, *History of the Crusades*, I, p. 159; C. R. Conder, *Latin Kingdom of Jerusalem*, p. 39.

52  The several MSS. give different readings. The kingdom reached to the Taurus mountains and the Sultanate of Rum or Iconium.

53  Beazley remarks that Benjamin must have passed along this coast before 1167, when Thoros died at peace and on terms of vassalage to the Emperor Manuel Comnenus. Malmistras is forty-five miles from Tarsus. Both had been recaptured by Manuel in 1155. *Josippon*, I, chap. i, identifies Tarshish with Tarsus.

54  No doubt the river Fer, otherwise Orontes, is here referred to. Ancient Antioch lies on the slope of Mount Silpius, and the city-wall erected by Justinian extended from the river up to the hill-plateau. Abulfeda says: "The river of Hamâh is also called Al Urunt or the Nahr al Maklûb (the Overturned) on account of its course from south to north; or, again, it is called Al' Âsi (the Rebel), for the reason that though most rivers water the lands on their borders without the aid of water-wheels, the river of Hamâh will not irrigate the lands except by the aid of machines for raising its waters." (Guy le Strange, *Palestine under the Moslems*, p. 59.) It is strange that R. Benjamin should call the Orontes the river Jabbok, but he always takes care to add that it rises in the Lebanon, to avoid any misconception that the Jabbok which falls into the Jordan is meant.

55  Boemond III, surnamed le Baube (the Stammerer), succeeded his mother in 1163. We owe the doubtless correct rendering of this passage to the ingenuity of the late Joseph Zedner. Benjamin visited Antioch before 1170, when a fearful earthquake destroyed a great part of the city.

56  It must be inferred from the context here, as well as from other passages, that when Benjamin mentions the number of Jews residing at a particular place he refers to the heads of families.

57  Gebal is the Gabala of ancient geographers. See Schechter, *Saadyana*, p. 25. Many travellers, among them Robinson, identify Baal-Gad with Banias, others suppose it to be Hasbeya.

58    Hashishim—hemp-smokers—hence is derived the word "assassin." See Socin, *Palestine and Syria*, pp. 68 and 99. Ibn Batuta and other Arabic writers have much to say about the Assassins or Mulahids, as they call them. They are again referred to by Benjamin on p. 54, where he states that in Persia they haunted the mountainous district of Mulahid, under the sway of the Old Man of the Mountain. The manner in which the Sheik acquired influence over his followers is amusingly described by Marco Polo (*The Book of Ser Marco Polo*: translated and edited by Colonel Sir Henry Yule; third edition, London, John Murray, 1903): "In a fertile and sequestered valley he placed every conceivable thing pleasant to man—luxurious palaces, delightful gardens, fair damsels skilled in music, dancing, and song, in short, a veritable paradise! When desirous of sending any of his band on some hazardous enterprise the Old Man would drug them and place them while unconscious in this glorious valley. But it was not for many days that they were allowed to revel in the joys of paradise. Another potion was given to them, and when the young men awoke they found themselves in the presence of the Old Man of the Mountain. In the hope of again possessing the joys of paradise they were ready to embark upon any desperate errand commanded by the Old Man." Marco Polo mentions that the Old Man found crafty deputies, who with their followers settled in parts of Syria and Kurdistan. He adds that, in the year 1252, Alaü, lord of the Tartars of the Levant, made war against the Old Man, and slaughtered him with many of his followers. Yule gives a long list of murders or attempts at murder ascribed to the Assassins. Saladin's life was attempted in 1174-6. Prince Edward of England was slain at Acre in 1172. The sect is not quite extinct. They have spread to Bombay and Zanzibar, and number in Western India over 50,000. The mention of the Old Man of the Mountain will

recall to the reader the story of Sinbad the Sailor in *The Arabian Nights*.

59 See Parchi, *Caphtor wa-pherach*, an exhaustive work on Palestine written 1322, especially chap. xi. The author spent over seven years in exploring the country.

60 Socin, the author of Baedeker's *Handbook to Palestine and Syria*, p. 557, gives the year of the earthquake 1157. It is referred to again p. 31. There was a very severe earthquake in this district also in 1170, and the fact that Benjamin does not refer to it furnishes us with another *terminus ad quem*.

61 See the narrative of William of Tyre.

62 Gubail, the ancient Gebal, was noted for its artificers and stonecutters. Cf. I Kings v. 32; Ezek. xxvii. 9. The Greeks named the place Byblos, the birthplace of Philo. The coins of Byblos have a representation of the Temple of Astarte. All along the coast we find remains of the worship of Baal Kronos and Baaltis, of Osiris and Isis, and it is probable that the worship of Adonis and Jupiter-Ammon led Benjamin to associate therewith the Ammonites. The reference to the children of Ammon is based on a misunderstanding, arising perhaps out of Ps. lxxxiii. 8.

63 *The Quarterly Statements of the Palestine Exploration Fund* for 1886 and 1889 give a good deal of information concerning the religion of the Druses. Their morality is there described as having been much maligned.

64 Tyre was noted for its glass-ware and sugar factories up to 1291, when it was abandoned by the Crusaders, and destroyed by the Moslems.

65 This name is applied to the Kishon, mentioned further on, celebrated in Deborah's song (Judg. v. 21), but it is about five miles south of Acre, the river nearest to the town being the Belus, noted for its fine sand suitable for glass-making. It is not unlikely that R. Benjamin alludes to the celebrated ox-spring of which

Arab writers have much to say. Mukkadasi writes in 985: "Outside the eastern city gate is a spring. This they call Ain al Bakar, relating how it was Adam—peace be upon him!—who discovered this spring, and gave his oxen water therefrom, whence its name."

66 Gath-Hepher, the birthplace of Jonah, near Kefr Kenna, in the territory of Zebulon (Joshua xix. 13), is not here referred to, but the land of Hepher, I Kings iv. 10 is probably meant.

67 In Benjamin's time hermits, who eventually founded the Carmelite order of monks, occupied grottoes on Mount Carmel.

68 Benjamin travelled along the coast to Caesarea. Mr. Guy Le Strange (*Palestine under the Moslems*, 1890, p. 477) writes: "Tall Kanîsah, or Al Kunaisah, the Little Church, is the mound a few miles north of Athlith, which the Crusaders took to be the site of Capernaum." Benjamin must have known very well that Maon, which was contiguous to another Carmel (referred to in Joshua xv. 55), belonged to Judah, and was not in the north of Palestine. Here, as in the case of Gath and elsewhere, he quotes what was the hearsay identification current at the time he visited these places. See an article by C.R. Conder on "Early Christian Topography" in the *Quarterly Statements of the Palestine Exploration Fund* for 1876, p.16. Cf. *The Ancient Hebrew Tradition*, by Prof. Fr. Hommel, p. 243.

69 In the time of the Crusaders Gath was supposed to be near Jamnia, but nothing definite is known as to its site. (Baedeker, *Handbook to Palestine and Syria*, 1876, p. 317.)

70 It lies between Caesarea and Lydda. See Conder's *Latin Kingdom of Jerusalem*. Munk's *Palestine* might also be consulted with advantage.

71 The tomb of St. George is still shown in the Greek church at Lydda.

72 Mr. A. Cowley in an article on the Samaritan Liturgy in *J. Q. R.*, VII, 125, states that the "House of Aaron" died out in 1624.

The office then went to another branch, the priest being called כהן הלוי , the Levite Cohon. Cf. Adler and Seligsohn's *Une nouvelle chronique Samaritaine.* (Paris: Durlacher, 1903.)

73  The small square building known as Joseph's tomb lies a short distance north of Jacob's well, at the eastern entrance to the vale of Nablous.

74  Cf. Guy Le Strange, *Palestine*, 381, and Rapoport's Note 166, Asher's *Benjamin*, vol. II, p. 87.

75  The MSS. are defective here; starting from Shechem, Mount Gilboa, which to this day presents a bare appearance, is in a different direction to Ajalon. It is doubtful whether Benjamin personally visited all the places mentioned in his *Itinerary*. His visit took place not long after the second great Crusade, when Palestine under the kings of Jerusalem was disturbed by internal dissensions and the onslaughts of the Saracens under Nur-ed-din of Damascus and his generals. Benjamin could at best visit the places of note only when the opportunity offered.

76  This and most of the other places mentioned by Benjamin are more or less identified in the very important work published by the Palestine Exploration Fund, *The Survey of Western Palestine.* Our author's statements are carefully examined, and Colonel Conder, after expatiating upon the extraordinary mistakes made by writers in the time of the Crusaders, some of whom actually confounded the sea of Galilee with the Mediterranean, says: "The mediæval Jewish pilgrims appear as a rule to have had a much more accurate knowledge both of the country and of the Bible. Their assertions are borne out by existing remains, and are of the greatest value."

77  King Baldwin III died in 1162, and was succeeded by his brother Almaric.

78  The reading of the Roman MS. that there were but four Jewish inhabitants at Jerusalem is in conformity with R. Pethachia, who passed through Palestine some ten or twenty years after R.

Benjamin, and found but one Jew there. The ד daleth meaning four would easily be misread for ר resh meaning 200.

79   The Knights of the Hospital of St. John and the Templars are here referred to. See Gibbon, *Decline and Fall of the Roman Empire*; Charles Mills, *History of the Crusades*, 4th edition, vol. I, p. 342, and Besant and Palmer's *Jerusalem*, chap. ix.

80   Cf. the writings of Mukaddasi the Hierosolomite, one of the publications of the Palestine Pilgrims' Text Society. See also Edrisi's and Ali of Herat's works. Chap. iii of Guy Le Strange's *Palestine* gives full extracts of Edrisi's account written in 1154 and Ali's in 1173. See also five plans of Jerusalem designed between 1160 and 1180, vol. XV, *Zeitschrift des Deutschen Palästina-Vereins*.

81   Ezek. xx. 35. The idea that the Gorge of Jehoshaphat will be the scene of the last judgment is based upon Joel iv. 2. Cf. M. N. Adler, *Temple at Jerusalem* and Sir Charles Warren's Comments.

82   In memory of Absalom's disobedience to his father, it is customary with the Jews to pelt this monument with stones to the present day. The adjoining tomb is traditionally known as that of Zechariah, 2 Chron. xxiv. 20, King Uzziah, otherwise Azariah, was buried on Mount Zion, close to the other kings of Judah, 2 Kings xv. 7. Cf. P. E. F., *Jerusalem*, as to identification of sites. Sir Charles Wilson, *Picturesque Palestine*, gives excellent illustrations of the holy places, and his work might be consulted with advantage.

83   Pillars of salt are to be met with elsewhere, for instance at Hammam Meskutim in Algeria. They are caused by spouts of water, in which so great a quantity of salt is contained as at times to stop up the aperture of the spring. The latter, however, is again unsealed through cattle licking off the salt near the aperture, and the same process of filling up and unstopping goes on continually. Cf. Talmud Berachot, 54 a.

84 See Baedeker's *Palestine and Syria*, pp. 233, 236; also Schwartz, *Palestine*, 1852, p. 230 and Dr. Robinson's *Palestine*, I, p. 516.

85 Edrisi in 1154 writes: "The tomb is covered by twelve stones, and above it is a dome vaulted over with stones."

86 Compare R. Pethachia's account of his visit (*Travels of Rabbi Petachia*: translated by Dr. A. Benisch; London, Trübner & Co., 1856, p. 63). See papers by Professors Goldziher and Guthe (*Zeitschrift des Deutschen Palästina-Vereins*, XVII, pp. 115 and 238) for an account of the opening of the tombs at Hebron in 1119, as given in a presumably contemporaneous MS. found by Count Riant. Fifteen earthenware vessels filled with bones, perhaps those referred to by Benjamin, were found. It is doubtful whether the actual tombs of the Patriarchs were disturbed, but it is stated that the Abbot of St. Gallen paid in 1180 ten marks of gold (equal to about £5,240 sterling) for relics taken from the altar of the church at Hebron. The MS. of Count Riant further mentions that before the occupation of Hebron by the Arabs, the Greeks had blocked up and concealed the entrance to the caves. The Jews subsequently disclosed the place of the entrance to the Moslems, receiving as recompense permission to build a synagogue close by. This was no doubt the Jewish place of worship referred to by Benjamin. Shortly after Benjamin's visit in 1167 the Crusaders established a bishopric and erected a church in the southern part of the Haram. See also Conder's account of the visit of His Majesty the King, when Prince of Wales, to the Haram at Hebron. (*Palestine Exploration Fund's Quarterly Statement*, 1882.)

87 Beit Jibrin was fortified by King Fulk in 1134. See Baedeker's *Palestine and Syria*, p. 309; Rapoport's *Erech Milin*, p. 54; also a preliminary notice on the Necropolis of Maresha in *P.E.F.Q.S.*, Oct., 1902, p. 393. The text has לגי , but it should be לבית . Inscriptions on tombs near Beit Jibrin show that the town, to

which those buried belonged, was called Mariseh. The passage in A and all printed editions as to Shunem and Toron de Los Caballeros is corrupt. Shunem was a small place in Galilee, and is not likely to have had 300 Jews at the time of the Crusaders, still less so Toron the present Latrun.

88 Shiloh, at the time of the Crusaders, was considered to occupy the site of Mizpeh, the highest mountain near Jerusalem, where the national assemblies were held at the time of the Judges. The present mosque is dilapidated, but the substructure, which dates from the Frank period, is beautifully jointed. The apse is raised. The reputed tomb of Samuel is on the western side of the church. It is still called Nebi Samwil, venerated alike by Jew and Moslem.

89 This and Mahomerie-le-grand, already mentioned, are Crusaders' churches. See Rey, *Les Colonies franques de Syrie aux XII'e et XIII'e siècles*, p. 387; also Conder, *The Latin Kingdom of Jerusalem*.

90 Beit-Nuba near Ramleh has been identified without proof with Nob. Richard Coeur-de-Lion encamped here some twenty-five years after Benjamin's visit. He with the army of the Crusaders passed through Ibelin on his way to Askelon. Cf. Vinsauf's *Itinerarium Regis Ricardi*.

91 See an interesting Paper, "Der Pass von Michmas," by Prof. D.G. Dalman, *Z.D.P.V.*, 1904, vol. XXVII, p. 161.

92 Asher renders רמיש Ramleh, for which there is some justification. Ramleh did not exist in Bible times—it was founded in 716. It prospered to such an extent that it became as large as Jerusalem. It was a good deal damaged by an earthquake in 1033. Ramleh had a large Moslem population, and the Jews there remained comparatively unmolested by the Crusaders. This latter fact accounts for the somewhat large number of Jews residing there. Asher's reading, and that of all the printed editions, is "about three Jews dwell there." This is obviously wrong. Probably the

copyist is to blame in taking ׳ש to be an abbreviation for שׁמ״ש. The reports of contemporary Arabic authors will be found in Guy Le Strange's *Palestine*, pp. 303-8.

93 Ali of Herat, Benjamin's contemporary, writes: "Askelon is a fine and beautiful city. There is near here the well of Abraham, which they say he dug with his own hand." Bohadin, in his *Life of Saladin*, gives a detailed account of the demolition of the city in 1192, after the conclusion of peace between King Richard I and Saladin. Ibn Batutah in 1355 found the town in ruins, but gives a detailed account of the well. (Guy Le Strange, pp. 402-3; cf. Dr. H. Hildesheimer, *Beiträge zur Geographie Palästinas*.)

94 The cathedral at Lydda with the tomb of St. George was destroyed when Saladin captured the place in 1191. It was rebuilt by a King of England in the seventeenth century.

95 A. M. Lunez in his Year-book for 1881, pp. 71-165, gives a complete list of the reputed Jewish tombs in Palestine. There are many records of the graves of Jewish worthies in our literature, but it is not easy to reconcile the different versions. See Jacob ben Nethanel's Itinerary given in Lunez's *Jerusalem*, 1906, VII, p. 87.

96 Both BM. and R have ר׳ יהודה הלוי, whilst E and A have the faulty reading ר׳ יהותה בן לוי. The Seder Hadoroth has the same reading as E and A. Jehuda Halevi died about thirty years before Benjamin's visit, and the question of the burial-place of our great national poet is thus finally settled.

97 The common belief is that Simon the Just was buried near Jerusalem, on the road to Nablous, about a mile from the Damascus Gate.

98 Cf. Schechter's *Saadyana*, p. 89.

99 The passage referring to the Arnon is evidently out of place.

100 See Deut. xi. 24.

101 For a description of the city and its great mosque, see Baedeker, also Guy Le Strange, *Palestine under the Moslems*, chap. vi. The most eastern dome of the mosque is to this day called Kubbet-es-Saa, the Dome of Hours. Mukaddasi gives an elaborate description of the mosaics and other features of this mosque.

102 Cf. *Midrash Raba*, chap, xiv:
אמר ר' לוי ואדם הגדול בענקים זה אברהם ; also Josephus, *Ant.* I, vii, 2 who quotes Nicolaus of Damascus in the words "*In Damasco regnarit Abramus.*"

103 Pethachia estimates the Jewish population at 19,000. This confirms the opinion already given (p. 26) that Benjamin refers to heads of families.

104 Dr. W. Bacher with justice observes that, at the time of the Crusades, the traditions of the Palestinian Gaonate seem to have survived at Damascus. See *J. Q. R.*, XV, pp. 79-96.

105 Galid as a city cannot be identified. Salchah is in the Eastern Hauran, half a day's journey from Bosra, and is spoken of in Scripture as a frontier city of Bashan. (Deut. iii. 10; Joshua xii. 5.) It lies a long way to the south of Damascus, whilst Baalbec lies to the north.

106 Tarmod is Tadmor or Palmyra.

107 The important city Emesa, now called Homs, is here probably indicated. In scripture, Gen. x. 18, the Zemarite and the Hamathite are grouped together among the Canaanite families. In this district is the intermittent spring of Fuwâr ed-Der, the Sabbatio River of antiquity, which Titus visited after the destruction of Jerusalem. Josephus (*Wars of the Jews*, Book VII, sec. 5) describes it as follows: "Its current is strong and has plenty of water; after which its springs fail for six days together and leave its channels dry, as any one may see; after which days it runs on the seventh day as it did before, and as though it had undergone no change at all: it has also been observed to keep this order perpetually and

exactly." The intermittent action is readily accounted for by the stream having hollowed out an underground duct, which acts as a syphon.

108  Hamath is often mentioned in Scripture, situated at no great distance from the Orontes. In the troublous time after the first crusade it was taken by the Ismailians or Assassins. The earthquake of 1157 caused great damage. Twenty years later the place was captured by Saladin.

109  Robinson and Conder identify Hazor with a site near Kedesh Naftali, but Sheiza is doubtless Sheizár, the ancient Larissa. Having regard to the readings of the other MSS., there is no doubt that Latmin, the next stage on the way to Aleppo, is the correct name of the place. See M. Hartmann's articles, "Beiträge zur Kenntuis der Syrischen Steppe," *Z.D.P.V.*, vols. XXII and XXIII, 1900 I. Cf. the article on the Boundaries of Palestine and Syria by M. Friedmann, Luncz's *Jerusalem*, vol. II.

110  Edrisi writes that there was abundance of water at Aleppo, but there is no discrepancy between Benjamin's and Edrisi's statements, as Asher supposes. The old waterworks were restored by Malek about the year 1200, some thirty years after Benjamin's visit.

111  Edrisi and Abulfeda speak of Balis and Kalat Jabar. See Guy Le Strange, p. 417. Zengy the Atabeg was slain at Kalat Jabar.

112  Rakka is on the left bank of the Euphrates. It was an important city of Upper Mesopotamia, commanding the Syrian frontier. Salchah is in the Hauran. See p. 30, note 5. On the right bank of the Euphrates, nearly opposite to Rakka, was Thapsacus. Here Cyrus forded the river, and here Alexander crossed in pursuit of Darius.

113  Harrân, the city of Nahor, is twenty-four miles SSE. of Edessa on the Balikh. Mustawfi tells us of Abraham's Shrine.

114 Ras-el-Ain, probably Rhesaina. The river Khabur—the Araxes of Xenophon—flows from the Kurdistan mountains southwards, and runs into the Euphrates.

115 The Gozan river cannot be, as tacitly assumed by Asher, the Kizil Uzun (also known as the Araxes). The Kizil Uzun is on the right of the watershed of the mountains of Kurdistan, and falls into the Caspian Sea. The Khabur above referred to flows through Mesopotamia, not through Media. The misconception arises probably from the author being too mindful of the passage occurring repeatedly in Scripture, e. g. 2 Kings xvii. 6: " . . . and placed them in Halah and in Habor by the river of Gozan, and in the cities of the Medes."

116 All the MSS. except BM. have here: "Thence it is two days to the city of Nisibis (Nasibin). This is a great city with rivulets of water, and contains about 1,000 Jews."

117 Josephus (*Antiquities*, I, 3) mentions that Noah's Ark still existed in his day. Rabbi Pethachia, who travelled through Armenia within twenty years after Benjamin, speaks of four mountain peaks, between which the Ark became fixed and from which it could not get free. Arab writers tell us that Jabal Judi (Koran, ch. xi, ver. 46) with the Mosque of Noah on the summit, could be seen from Geziret. See also *Marco Polo*, Bk. I. ch. 3.

118 See Lebrecht's Essay "On the State of the Caliphate at Bagdad." Sin-ed-din, otherwise known as Seif-ed-din, died 1149, some twenty years before Benjamin's visit, and Graetz (vol. VI, note 10) suggests that the appointment of Astronomer Royal must have been made by Nur-ed-din's nephew. None of the MSS. have this reading, nor is such a correction needed. R. Joseph may have been appointed by Nur-ed-din's brother, and would naturally retain the office during the reign of his successor.

119 Irbil, or Arbela, is two days' journey from Mosul. See Saadyana, *J. Q. R.*, vol. XIV, p. 503, and W. Bacher's note, p. 741.

120 For a full account of Mosul and other places here referred to, see Mr. Guy Le Strange's *The Lands of the Eastern Caliphate*, 1905, also Layard's *Nineveh and its Remains* and *Nineveh and Babylon*. Layard carefully examined Nebbi Junus, which is held in great veneration by the Mussulmans, and came to the conclusion that the tradition which places Jonah's tomb on this spot is a mere fable (p. 596). It will be seen that Benjamin speaks of the Shrine as a *Synagogue*. At Alkush near Mosul the tomb of Nahum is pointed out, and the Arabs say that after Jonah had fulfilled his mission to the people of Nineveh they relapsed into idolatry. Then Nahum denounced the city and was slain by the populace, who proclaimed him and Jonah to be false prophets, since the doom the latter foretold does not come to pass, See Schwarz, *Das Heilige Land*, 1852, p. 259, identifying Kefar Tanchum near Tiberias with Nahum's burialplace

121 As to Jewish seats of learning in Babylon refer to Dr. Krauss's Article "Babylonia" in the *Jewish Encyclopaedia*; see also Guy Le Strange, p. 74, who suggests that Pumbedita means "mouth of the Badat canal." Cf. *J. Q. R.*, XVII, p. 756.

122 Hadara goes under the name Alhathr or Hatra. There must exist great doubt as to whether Benjamin had personally satisfied himself as to the Jewish population he gives for this and the other places he tells of, till he comes to Egypt. Up to this point the Traveller has always appeared to under-estimate the Jewish population. Henceforth it will be found that he gives apparently exaggerated figures,—and this lends colour to the view that Benjamin did not proceed beyond Ispahan, but found his way thence direct to Egypt. The statements concerning the intervening places must therefore be taken to have been based upon hearsay information. Pethachia's remarks are significant: "In the land of Cush and Babel are more than sixty myriads of Jews; as many are in the land of Persia. But in Persia the Jews are subject to hard bondage

and suffering. Therefore Rabbi Pethachia visited only one city in Persia." (Dr. Benisch's edition, p. 19.)

123 The Caliphs of the Abbaside Dynasty traced their descent from Mohammed. Benjamin here refers to the Caliph El Mostanshed. The Caliph is aptly compared to the Pope. In addition to his temporal authority at Bagdad, he exercised as Leader of the Faithful—Emir al-Muminin—religious authority over all Mohammedans from Spain to India. At a later time the vizier arrogated all authority to himself, and the Caliph spent his time either in the mosque or in the seraglio.

124 *Lebrecht*, p. 391, states that this was a scarf of black velvet, generally a portion of the hangings of the mosque of Mecca, which was suspended from a balcony of the Palace and was called the Sleeve of the Caliph.

125 The statements here made are strangely contradictory; see a suggestive article by Dr. Goldziher in *Z.D.P.V.*, 1905, p. 151.

126 A valuable work, *Bagdad during the Abbaside Caliphate, from Contemporary Arabic and Persian Sources*, appeared in 1900, written by Mr. Guy Le Strange, which helps to explain Benjamin's account of the Moslem metropolis. The Caliph Mansur in 762 selected it as the Capital of the Empire. Numerous references in the Talmud prove that a Jewish settlement was there long before. Mansur built a double-walled Round City two miles in diameter on the western side of the Tigris. It formed the nucleus of suburbs, which spread over both banks of the Tigris. A very fair idea of the metropolis may be obtained if we imagine the Round City as situated on the Surrey side of the Thames, having the "Elephant and Castle" for its centre. At this spot stood the great Mosque of Mansur, where the Friday services were held, and where the Caliph took a prominent part in the service on the Bairam, at the close of the Ramazan fast. The Round City being subject to periodical inundations, the government buildings were gradually transferred to the eastern

side of the river. The Royal Palaces, in the grounds called the Harim, which were fully three miles in extent, occupied the site similar to that from Westminster to the City. At one time there were as many as twenty-three palaces within the royal precincts. The Caliph, when visiting the Mosque in state, left the palace grounds, and proceeded over the main bridge, corresponding to Westminster Bridge, along a road which in Benjamin's time led to the Basrah Gate quarter. At the close of the ceremony in the Mosque, the Caliph returned, crossing the bridge of boats, and proceeded to his palace by a road corresponding to the Thames Embankment. The members of his court and the nobles entered barges and escorted him alongside the river.

The Arab writers mention that certain palaces were used as state prisons, in which the Caliphs kept their nearer relations in honourable confinement. They were duly attended by numerous servants, and amply supplied with every luxury, but forbidden under pain of death to go beyond the walls. Lebrecht, p. 381, explains the circumstances under which the Caliph Moktafi imprisoned his brother and several of his kinsmen. There were large hospitals in Bagdad: the one to which Benjamin alludes is the Birmaristan of the Mustansiriyah, in Western Bagdad, which for three centuries was a great school of medical science. Its ruins, close to the present bridge of boats, are still to be seen. The reader must bear in mind that at the time when Benjamin visited Bagdad, the Seljuk Sultans had been defeated, and the Caliphs stood higher than ever in power. They, however, took little interest in political affairs, which were left entirely in the hands of their viziers.

127 Asher and the other printed editions give the Jewish population at 1,000. Pethachia makes the same estimate, which, however, is inconsistent with his statement, that the Head of the Academy had 2,000 disciples at one time, and that more than 500 surrounded him.

The British Museum and Casanatense MSS. solve the difficulty; they have the reading *forty thousand.* It would be wearisome to specify in these notes all the places where a superior reading is presented by these MSS.; the student will, however, find that not a few anomalies which confronted Asher are now removed.

128  The last or tenth Academy.

129  This appellation is applied in the Talmud to scholars who uninterruptedly apply themselves to communal work.

130  The first line of Exilarchs, which ended with Hezekiah in the year 1040, traced their descent from David through Zerubbabel. Hisdai's pedigree was through Hillel, who sprang from a female branch of the Royal line (see Graetz, vol. VI, note 10). Pethachia writes (p. 17) that a year before his arrival at Bagdad Daniel died. A nephew, David, became Exilarch jointly with R. Samuel, the Head of the great Academy, whose authority over all the communities in Asia became paramount. Samuel had an only daughter, who was learned in the Scriptures and the Talmud. She gave instruction through a window, remaining in the house, whilst the disciples were below, unable to see her.

131  The office of Exilarch had but recently been revived, and the Mohammed here referred to may have been Mohammed El Moktafi, the Caliph Mostanshed's predecessor.

132  The Alans throughout the Middle Ages occupied Georgia and the regions of the Caucasus. As to the Iron Gates which Alexander made, Yule in commenting on Marco Polo's text (*Travels of Ser Marco Polo:* edited by Sir Henry Yule, 3rd edition, London, John Murray, chap, iii) says that Benjamin was the first European traveller to mention this pass. Benjamin and Marco Polo both record the general belief currrent at the time that the Pass of Derbend was traversed by Alexander. It is still called in Turkish "Demis-Kapi" or the Iron Gate, and the Persians designate it "Sadd-i-Iskandar"—the Rampart of Alexander. Lord Curzon,

however, in his valuable work *Persia and the Persians*, vol. 1, p. 293, proves conclusively that the pass through which Alexander's army marched when pursuing Darius after the battle of Arbela could not have been at Derbend. Arrian, the historian of Alexander's expeditions, writes that the pass was one day's journey from Rages (the noted city mentioned in the Book of Tobit) for a man marching at the pace of Alexander's army. But Derbend is fully 500 miles from Rages. In Lord Curzon's opinion, confirmed by Spiegel, Droysen and Schindler, the Sirdara Pass, some forty miles from Teheran on the way to Meshed, must have been the defile which Alexander's army forced. I think it will be found that Marco Polo's geography is less reliable than that of Benjamin. In the third chapter referred to above, Marco Polo speaks of the Euphrates falling into the Caspian Sea.

133 Probably the Oxus, called by the Arabs "Gaihun." Rabad I, a contemporary of Benjamin, speaks of the land of Gurgan in his Sefer Hakabalah. The Nestorian Christians are probably here referred to.

134 It is interesting to compare this account with that of the Installation of the Egyptian Nagid (*J.Q.R.*, IX, p. 717).

135 This is a well-known sage, whose name often occurs in the Talmud.

136 The Babel of Bible times was captured by Sennacherib; after stopping up a dam of the Euphrates, the country was placed under water and the city destroyed. Nebuchadnezzar restored the city; he also erected a magnificent palace for himself—the Kasr— also the Temple of Bel. Herodotus, Book I, chaps. 178-89, fully describes these edifices, and dwells upon the huge extent of the metropolis, which was estimated to have a circuit of fifty miles. Xerxes destroyed the city. Alexander the Great contemplated the restoration of Bel's Temple, but as it would have taken two months for 10,000 men merely to remove the rubbish, he abandoned the

attempt. The ruins have been recently explored by Germans. The embankments which regulated the flow of the Euphrates and Tigris have given way, and at the present time the whole region round Babylon is marshy and malarious. In the words of Jeremiah, li. 43, "Her cities are a desolation, a sterile land, and a wilderness, a place wherein no man dwelleth."

137 The Valley of Dura mentioned in Daniel iii. is here referred to. See Dr. Berliner's *Beiträge zur Geographie und Ethnographie Babyloniens*; also Layard's *Nineveh and Babylon*, p. 469. Cf. Berachot, 57 b.

138 Bereshith Rabba, chap. xxxviii, says the tower was at Borsippa, and the ruins here spoken of are probably those of the Birs Nimroud, fully described by Layard, *Nineveh and Babylon*, chap, xxii, p. 496. He says: "The mound rises abruptly to the height of 198 feet, and has on its summit a compact mass of brickwork 37 feet high by 28 broad ... On one side of it, beneath the crowning masonry, lie huge fragments torn from the pile itself. The calcined and vitreous surface of the bricks, fused into rock-like masses, show that their fall may have been caused by lightning. The ruin is rent almost from top to bottom. No traces whatever now remain of the spiral passage spoken of by the Jewish traveller." Cf. Professor T. K. Cheyne's article, "The Tower of Babel," in the new *Biblical Cyclopaedia*. Nebuchadnezzar, in his Borsippa inscription, records that the tower, which had never originally been completed, had fallen into decay, and that the kiln-bricks had split. These are the Agur bricks mentioned by Benjamin; cf. Isaiah xxvii. 9. Al-ajur is the word still used by the Arabs for kiln-burnt bricks.

139 Niebuhr, vol. II, 216, gives a full account of his visit to the tomb. Layard, speaking of Birs Nimroud, says: "To the southwest in the extreme distance rise the palm-trees of Kifil, casting their scanty shade over a small dome, the tomb of Ezekiel. To this spot occasionally flock in crowds, as their forefathers have done for centuries, the Jews of Bagdad, Hillah, and other cities

of Chaldea ... It is now but a plain building, despoiled of the ornaments and MSS. which it once appears to have contained" (*Nineveh and Babylon*, p. 500). Alcharizi composed a beautiful ode when visiting this tomb (chap, xxxv, also chap. L).

140 This Mohammed, as in the case referred to p. 40, must have been a predecessor of the reigning Caliph, as the Prophet was never in Babylonia, and in no case would he have granted favours to the Jews. It should be noted that the British Museum MS. on which our text is based, as well as the Casanatense MS., generally styles the Prophet המשוגע. The MS., on which the Constantinople *editio princeps* is based, had probably all passages where this epithet or other objectionable remarks were used excised by the censor, and it will be seen that the passage before us, with reference to the grant of land by Mohammed, as well as that further on, referring to Ali, the son-in-law of Mohammed, do not appear in any of the printed editions. Dr. Hirschfeld is of opinion that, on the one hand, the epithet is the translation of the Arabic *majnūn*, a term against which Mohammed protested several times in the Koran, because it means he was possessed by a *jinn*, like a soothsayer. On the other hand, the word was chosen having regard to Hosea ix. 7. This was done long before Benjamin's time, by Jafeth and others.

141 See picture of the traditional tomb of Ezekiel in the *Jewish Encyclopaedia*, vol. V, p. 315.

142 The Talmud (Sabbath, II a) speaks of the destruction of Mata Mehasya. Sura took its place as a centre of learning.

143 See Berliner, pp. 45, 47, 54, and 57, for particulars derived from the Talmud and Midrash as to the several centres of Jewish learning in Babylonia.

144 This synagogue is repeatedly mentioned in the Talmud. Zunz (Note 255) omits mentioning Aboda Zarah, 43 b, where Rashi

explains that Shafjathib was a place in the district of Nehardea, and that Jeconiah and his followers brought the holy earth thither, giving effect to the words of the Psalmist: "For thy servants take pleasure in her stones, and favour the dust thereof" (Ps. cii. 14).

145 Benjamin visited the various seats of learning in the neighbourhood, and thus came again to Nehardea, which has been already mentioned on p. 34. Rab Jehuda, not Rab, is there associated with Samuel.

146 Asher, at this stage of Benjamin's narrative, has the following note: "For the illustration of that portion of our text which treats of Arabia, we refer the reader to the Rev. S.L. Rapoport's paper, 'Independent Jews of Arabia,' which will be found at the end of these notes." No such account appeared in the work, but in the *Bikkure Haittim* for the year 1824, p. 51, there appears an interesting essay in Hebrew on the subject by Rapoport, to which the reader is referred. It is a matter of history that the powerful independent Jewish communities which were settled at Yathrib, afterwards called Medina, and in the volcanic highlands of Kheibar and Teima called the Harrah, were crushed by Mohammed. Dr. Hirschfeld, in the *Jewish Quarterly Review*, vol. XV, p. 170, gives us the translation of a letter found in the Cairo *Genizah*, addressed by Mohammed to the people of Kheibar and Maqna, granting them certain privileges from which the Jews, who were allowed to remain in their homes, benefited. Omar, the second Caliph, broke the compact, but allowed them to settle at Kufa on the Euphrates. Although pilgrims pass annually up and down the caravan tracks to Mecca, the information respecting the old Jewish sites in the Harrah is most meagre. Edrisi and Abulfeda throw no light on Benjamin's account. In the year 1904 an able work by Mr. D.G. Hogarth appeared under the title of *The Penetration of Arabia*, being a record of the development of Western knowledge concerning the Arabian Peninsula. He gives a full account of the European

travellers who have described the country. Niebuhr, who visited Yemen in 1762, repeated the statement made by the Italian traveller Varthema that there were still wild Jews in Kheibar. The missionary Joseph Woolf visited Arabia in 1836, and he gives us an account of an interview he had with some of the Rechabites. No weight, however, can be attached to his fantastic stories. W.G. Palgrave, who resided for some years in Syria as a Jesuit, where he called himself Father Michael (Cohen), was entrusted in 1862 with a mission to Arabia by Napoleon III in connexion with the projected Suez Canal; he was one of the few visitors to the Harrah, but he makes no special reference to the Jews. Joseph Halevi made many valuable discoveries of inscriptions in South Arabia, which he traversed in 1869. He visited the oppressed Jewish community at Sanaa in Yemen; he further discovered traces of the ancient Minaean kingdom, and found that the Jews in the Nejran were treated with singular tolerance and even favour; but he was not able to tell us anything respecting the Jews of the Harrah.

C.M. Doughty was, however, more successful when visiting this district in 1875. Of Kheibar he says "that it is now a poor village whose inhabitants are a terrible kindred, Moslems outwardly, but, in secret, cruel Jews that will suffer no stranger to enter among them." See C.M. Doughty's *Arabia Deserta*, vol. II, p. 129. "Teima is a Nejd colony of Shammar; their fathers came to settle there not above 200 years past. Old Teima of the Jews, according to their tradition, had been (twice) destroyed by flood. From those times there remain some great rude stone buildings. It is now a prosperous open place" (vol. I, p. 286).

The only writer that casts any doubt upon Benjamin's record as to independent Jewish tribes in Arabia is R. Jacob Safir, who visited Yemen and other Arabian ports in the Red Sea in the year 1864. See chaps. xv and xliii of *Iben Safir*, Lyck, 1866. Dr. L.

Grünhut, in his introduction, *Die Reisebeschreibungen des R. Benjamin von Tudela*, Jerusalem, 1903, p. 16, refutes Safir's statements.

In Hogarth's work, p. 282, is shown a print of the Teima stone, with its Aramaic inscription, considered to belong to the fourth or fifth century B.C., and on p. 285 will be found Doughty's interesting sketch of Kheibar.

147 It is clear that, when speaking of the population of some of these places, the whole oasis or district is intended, and not a particular town.

148 In reading through the foregoing account of the Jews in Arabia, it is quite clear that Benjamin never visited the country, nor did he pretend to have done so. In the words of Mr. C. E. Beazley (The Dawn of Modern Geography, p. 252), "It is no longer, for the most part, a record of personal travel; it is rather an attempt to supplement the first part 'of things seen' by a second 'of things heard.'" But Beazley is wrong when he characterizes as "wild" the account of the Jews of Southern Arabia "who were Rechabites." Does Benjamin say so? There is no such reading in the MS. of the British Museum. The student, it is thought, will by this time have come to the conclusion that it is the oldest and most trustworthy of our available authorities. The whole misconception has arisen from the fact that the unreliable MS. E and all the printed editions have transposed the letters of ביבר and made רכב of it. Rapoport, in the article already referred to, seems to suspect the faulty reading: to justify it, he connects the men of Kheibar with the Rechabites and the sons of Heber the Kenite, basing his argument upon Jer. xxxv, Judges i. 16, I Sam. xxvii. 10, and I Chron. ii. 55.

Neither Zunz nor Asher makes any comments upon this chapter of the itinerary. Graetz gives an abstract of Benjamin's account; he, as well as all other writers, is unable to identify Tilmas, but is of opinion that Tanai must be Sanaa, the capital of Yemen, which, however, is twenty-five days' journey beyond Kheibar. It is well known that Yemen has, since Bible times, harboured a Jewish population, who—notwithstanding all oppression, intensified under Turkish rule—inhabit many of its towns and villages to the present day. It is comparatively accessible, owing to its proximity to the sea. We must cherish the hope that Great Britain, now that it claims the Hinterland of Aden, will extend its protection to the Jews.

The volcanic highlands (Harrah) of Kheibar were always inaccessible, owing to their being surrounded by waterless deserts and fanatic Bedouin tribes.

R. Abraham Farissol, who flourished at the beginning of the sixteenth century, writes that there was a large number of Jews in the district, who lived in tents and in wooden houses or huts. His contemporary, David Reubeni, who crossed from Arabia to Abyssinia and came to Europe in 1524, pretended to be brother of Joseph, king of the tribes of Reuben, Gad, and half-Manasseh in the desert of Chabor (Kheibar). Benjamin takes care to qualify his statement as to the origin of the Jews of Kheibar by adding ואומרים בני אדם— —"*people say* they belong to the tribes of Reuben, Gad, and the half-tribe of Manasseh, whom Salmanesser, King of Assyria, led hither into captivity."

I would here mention an interesting work of Dr. R. Dozy, Professor of History and Oriental Languages at Leyden, *Die Israeliten in Mecca*, 1864. By a series of ingenious inferences from Bible texts (1 Sam. xxx, 1 Chron. iv. 24-43, &c.) he essays to establish that the tribe of Simeon, after David had dispersed the Amalekites who had already been weakened by Saul, entered Arabia and settled all along in the land of the Minaeans and at Mecca, where they established the worship at the Kaaba and introduced practices which have not been altogether abandoned up to the present day. Dr. Dozy further contends that after Hezekiah's reign numerous Jewish exiles came to Arabia.

Hommel, in two articles in Ersch and Gruber's *Encyclopaedia*, under "Bedouins" and "Anzah," gives full particulars respecting the Anizeh, otherwise Anaessi, tribe—that they were in the habit of joining the Wahabees and other Bedouin tribes in attacking caravans and levying blackmail. The Turkish Pasha at Damascus had to pay annually passage-money to ensure the safety of the pilgrims to Mecca. On one occasion two of the Bedouin sheiks were decoyed by the Turks and killed; but the Anaessi, aided by other tribes to the number of 80,000, took ample revenge by pillaging the Mecca caravan on its return. They seized a quantity of pearls, and the women were said to have attempted boiling them with the rice. Seetzen (*Journey through Syria, &c.*, I, ch. i, p. 356) says, "In Kheibar are no Jews now, only Anaessi." Layard and other modern writers often refer to the Anizeh Bedouins. Travellers go in dread of them in the Syrian desert and all along the Euphrates. Doughty mentions that they, more than any other tribe, resemble the Jews both in appearance and disposition.

Ritter (*Geographie*, vol. XII), in quoting Niebuhr, makes mention of the widespread Anizeh tribe of Bedouins who were anciently known to be Jews. He further states that the Jews of Damascus and Aleppo shun them as they are non-observant Jews, considered by some to be Karaites. Does all this give ground for any presumption that they are or were crypto-Jews, the descendants of the former Kheibar Jews, possibly also of those whom Omar allowed to settle at Kufa?

This lengthy note may be closed fitly with the following mysterious remark in Doughty's usual quaint style (vol. I, p. 127), in connexion with the murder of a Bagdad Jew who tried to reach Kheibar: "But let none any more jeopardy his life for Kheibar! I would that these leaves might save the blood of some: and God give me this reward of my labour! for who will, he may read in them all the tale of Kheibar."

149 It will be seen further on (p. 67) that Benjamin speaks of Aden as being in India, "which is on the mainland." It is well known that Abyssinia and Arabia were in the Middle Ages spoken of as "Middle India." It has been ascertained that in ancient times the Arabs extensively colonized the western sea-coast of the East Indies. Cf. the article "Arabia," in the ninth edition of the *Encyclopaedia Britannica* and Supplement.

150 The Casanatense MS. here interpolates: "Thence it takes seven days to Lusis, where there are 2,000 Israelites." Asher substitutes for Lusis Wasit, a place near the Tigris. I am unable to identify the river Virae, and the words "which is in the land of Al Yemen" are evidently out of place.

151 See Dr. Hartwig Hirschfeld's account of a Fragment of a Work by Judah Al-harizi, being a description of a pilgrimage through Mesopotamia with a view to visit Ezra's grave. The Arab geographer Yakut locates the grave in the village Maisan on the river Samara near the place where the Euphrates and Tigris unite (*J. Q. R.*, vol. XV, 683). Layard writes as follows:—"We stopped at the so-called tomb of the prophet Ezra, about twenty-five miles from the junction of the Tigris and Euphrates, at Korna. The building, which is of a comparatively modern date, consisted of two chambers, an outer one which was empty, and an inner one containing the tomb built of bricks, covered with white stucco and enclosed in a wooden case, over which was thrown a large blue cloth fringed with yellow tassels with the name of the donor embroidered on it in Hebrew characters. No trace of either the large synagogue or of the mosque mentioned by Benjamin now exists, and it may be doubted whether the present building covers the tomb which was seen by the Hebrew traveller. We could find no ancient remains near it, as the Tigris is constantly changing its

course, and was still eating away the bank of alluvial soil, upon the edge of which the building stood. It is highly probable that the tomb seen by Benjamin of Tudela had long before been carried away by the river." Layard's *Early Adventures in Persia, Susiana, and Babylonia*, vol. II, p. 214. See also an elaborate note of Dr. Benisch, p. 91 of his edition of Pethachia's Travels, and I. J. Benjamin II, *Eight Years in Asia and Africa*, p. 167.

152 As for the river Gozan see p. 33, n. 3, and p. 58, n. 4. The mountains of Chafton, referred to also in pp. 54, 55, would seem to include not only the Zagros range, but also the highlands of Kurdistan.

153 *Marco Polo*, book II, chap, xlv, says of Tibet: "In this country there are many of the animals that produce musk. The Tartars have great numbers of large and fine dogs which are of great service in catching the musk-beasts, and so they procure a great abundance of musk."

154 The reputed sepulchre of Daniel is situated between Schuster and Dizful in Persia, close by the river Shaour, an affluent of the Karun river, which is supposed to be the Ulai of the Bible, Dan. viii. 2. It is within sight of the vast mound which denotes the site of Susa, the ancient Shushan. Here Mme. Dieulafoy in 1881 made extensive excavations of the palace of the Persian kings, many relics of which are now on view at the Louvre in Paris.

The tomb of Daniel has been fully described by Layard—see *Early Adventures*, vol. II, p. 295. It is of comparatively recent date, not unlike the shrines of Mussulman saints, and is surmounted by a high conical dome of irregular brickwork, somewhat resembling in shape a pine cone. The reader is referred to the beautiful pictorial illustrations of Daniel's reputed tomb, of the ruins of Susa, and of Schuster and its bridges in Mme. Dieulafoy's *La Perse, la Chaldée et la Susiane*, Paris, 1887.

There is nothing to connect the building on the banks of the Shaour with the tomb of Daniel save the Mussulman tradition.

There are many legends connected with the reputed sepulchre, one of which is to the effect that the men of Susa diverted the river in order to bury Daniel's coffin in its bed. See Guy Le Strange, p. 240.

E.N. Adler, in his recent work *Jews in many Lands*, Jewish Historical Society of England, p. 224, in describing Samarkand, writes as follows: "Tradition has it that Tamerlane had seen the tomb at Susa in Persia, with a warning inscribed thereon, that none should open its door; and so he broke it open from behind, and found it written that Nebi Daniel was there buried. The impetuous conqueror had the sarcophagus removed with all reverence, and carried it with him to his own capital to be its palladium. The sarcophagus is over twenty yards long as beseems a prophet's stature. It has been recently covered by a brick chapel with three cupolas, but photographs of the ancient structure can be had in Samarkand. It is grandly placed at the edge of a cliff overhanging the rapid river Seop. The local Jews do not believe the story, nor do they quite disbelieve it, for I went with two who prayed there at the grave of the righteous."

155 The reader will recollect that reference to this sect has already been made on page 16. See Guy Le Strange, p. 220 and p. 354.

156 Amadia (Imadiyah) is a city in Kurdistan in a mountainous district, north of Mosul. Ben Virga and R. Joseph Hacohen, the author of *Emek Habacha*, state that 1,000 Jewish families lived in the city at that time. It is strange that in all the MSS., including Asher's text, this city is called Amaria instead of Amadia. The mistake doubtless arose from the fact that the copyists mistook the Hebrew letter 'resh' for a Hebrew letter 'daleth'. The scribe of the British Museum MS. had made other errors of this kind, writing בנראר for בנדאד, הרמוז for הרמוד, &c. See Guy Le Strange, p. 92.

157   The author of *Emek Habacha* gives the date of the Alroy tragedy as 1163. It should, however, be antedated by a few years. Benjamin must have passed through Egypt on his return journey some time before Sept., 1171. See note 2, p. 1. He here tells us that the Alroy catastrophe took place just ten years before his visit to Bagdad and the neighbourhood. It is clear therefore that 1160 is the latest date when this event could have taken place.

158   This Turkoman may have been the Prince of Arbela who in 1167 joined Saladin in his successful invasion of Egypt. He was remarkable for his great strength and courage (see Bohadin's *Life of Saladin*, Palestine Pilgrims' Text Society, p. 51).

159   The accounts given by Ben Virga in *Sheret Jehudah*, and by Joseph Hacohen in *Emek Habacha*, are evidently based upon Benjamin's record, and throw no fresh light on this Messianic movement. Asher, vol. II, note 300, promises but fails to give the contents of an Arabic document written by a contemporary, the renegade Samuel Ibn Abbas, which the savant S. Munk had discovered in the Paris library; a German translation of this document appears in Dr. Wiener's *Emek Habacha*, 1858, p. 169. The name of the pseudo-Messiah is given as Menahem, surnamed Al-Ruhi, but Munk satisfactorily proves that he is identical with our David Alroy. Being a young man of engaging appearance and great accomplishments, he gained considerable influence with the governor of Amadia, and had a considerable following among the Jews of Persia. With the intention of occupying the castle, he introduced a number of his armed adherents into the town, who were careful, however, to conceal their weapons. The governor detected the conspiracy, and put Alroy to death. The excitement among the Jews lasted for a considerable time. Two impostors, with letters purporting to emanate from Alroy, came to Bagdad, and worked upon the credulity of the community. Men and women parted with their money and jewellery, having been brought to

believe that on a certain night they would be able to fly on angels' wings from the roofs of their houses to Jerusalem. The only thing which made the women feel unhappy was the fear that their little ones might not be able to keep pace with them in the aerial flight. At daybreak the fraud was discovered, but the impostors had meanwhile decamped with their treasure. The chronicler adds that the year in which this occurred was called The Year of Flight.

De Sacy, in his *Chrestomathie Arabe*, I, p. 363, gives a similar story, the authorship of which he ascribes to Schahristani.

160  Asher, vol. II, p. 167, n. 304, gives expression to a keen desire for further particulars as to this tomb. Dr. J. E. Polak, formerly Physician to the late Shah of Persia, gives the desired information, on p. 26, in an interesting work on Persia. He writes as follows: "The only national monument which the Jews in Persia possess is the tomb of Esther at Hamadan, the ancient Ecbatana, whither they have made pilgrimages from time immemorial. In the centre of the Jewish quarter there is to be seen a low building with a cupola, on the top of which a stork has built its nest. The entrance is walled up for the greater part; there only remains below a small aperture which can be closed by a movable flat stone serving the purpose of a door and affording some protection from attacks, which are not uncommon. In the entrance hall, which has but a low ceiling, are recorded the names of pilgrims; also the year when the building was restored. Thence one gains access into a small four-cornered chamber in which there are two high sarcophagi made of oak, which are the monuments of Esther and Mordecai. On both of them are inscribed in Hebrew the words of the last chapter of the Book of Esther, as well as the names of three Physicians at whose expense the tomb was repaired." Dr. Polak states that in the Middle Ages the Jewish population of Persia was very large, especially in the southern provinces. In recent years it

has greatly diminished in consequence of dire persecution. He was assured that not more than 2,000 Jewish families remained in the country. Eighty years ago the entire community at Meshed were forcibly converted to Islam. Cf. E. N. Adler, *Jews in Many Lands*, p. 214.

161 Referring to Benjamin's statement that Mordecai and Esther are buried at Hamadan, an interesting article by Mr. Israel Abrahams upon the subject, with an illustration of the traditional tomb, as well as a picture of ancient Susa, will be found in the *Jewish Chronicle* of March 19, 1897. In the issue of March 4, 1898, Mr. Morris Cohen, of Bagdad, furnished a full copy of the inscriptions in the Mausoleum, but they possess no historical value. The reputed Prayer of Esther seen there by former travellers is no longer extant.

The statement of E. Jehiel Heilprin, in the *Seder Hadoroth*, that Mordecai and Esther are buried at Shomron is devoid of foundation, and may have arisen through reading here שמיר **for** הפרץ. For information derived from the works of mediaeval Arab writers respecting Persia and the adjacent countries the reader should consult Mr. Guy Le Strange's book, *The Lands of the Eastern Caliphate*. The maps will be found most useful.

162 The British Museum version omits this passage. An inspection of the map will show that Tabaristan lies a long distance to the north of the trade route which leads from Hamadan to Ispahan.

163 The great extent of Ispahan is accounted for by the fact that it consisted of two towns; the one called Jay, measured half a league across; the other, Al Yahudiyah, the "Jew Town" two miles to the westward, was double the size of Jay. Mukadassi states that the city had been originally founded by the Jews in the time of Nebuchadnezzar, because its climate resembled that of Jerusalem. Le Strange, p. 203.

164 Lord Curzon, in his work on Persia, devotes chap. xix in vol. II to a description of the City of Ispahan, and of his journey there. Chap. xx contains an account of his journey from Ispahan to Shiraz. The distance between the two cities is 81 parasangs, equivalent to 312 miles. It will be seen that here, as well as in the cases of Ghaznah, Samarkand, and Tibet, Benjamin altogether under-estimates the true distances.

165 Asher, following the printed editions, quotes the Jewish population of this place as 8,000, and assumes, without any justification, that Khiva is here referred to. He also substitutes Oxus for Gozan. In the Middle Ages the Oxus was known under the name of Jayhun or Gihon (Gen. ii. 13). The name of the city according to our text is Ghaznah, which eight hundred years ago was the capital of Afghanistan. Ibn Batuta says it was ten stages from Kandahar on the way to Herat. Le Strange (p. 348) writes as follows: "Ghaznah became famous in history at the beginning of the eleventh century as the capital of the great Mahmud of Ghaznah, who at one time was master both of India on the east and Bagdad on the west." Istakhri says: "No city of this countryside was richer in merchants and merchandise, for it was as the port of India." The river Gozan, on which we are told Ghaznah lies, must appear to the reader to be ubiquitous. On p. 33 we find the Habor of Kurdistan is its affluent; on p. 55 it is at Dabaristan; on p. 59 in Khorasan. There is a simple solution of the difficulty. In each of the localities Benjamin was told that the river was called Gozan; for in the Mongolian language "Usun" is the name for water or river. Thus "Kisil-Usun" means "Red River." The addition of a "g" before a "u" or "w" is quite a common feature in language; it occurs, for instance, in the Romance and Keltic languages.

166 The British Museum text has: "And he put them in Halah and in Habor and the mountains of Gozan and the mountains of the Medes." Having regard to the passages 2 Kings xix. 12 and

Isaiah xxxvii. 12, Nöldeke maintains that there was a tract of land watered by the river Gozan, known as Gozanitis, which Scripture refers to. See *J. Q. R.*, vol. I, p. 186.

Naisabur is a city near Meshed, and close to high mountains which are a continuation of the Elburz mountain range.

We draw attention to the cautious manner in which Benjamin speaks here and elsewhere when alluding to the whereabouts of any of the ten tribes. The tradition is widespread that independent Jewish tribes were to be found in Khorasan until recent times. Mr. E. N. Adler was told that in an Armenian monastery near Kutais, ancient records are preserved which conclusively prove that the Jews were paramount in certain districts three or four centuries ago; *Jews in many Lands*, p. 178. Cf. *Wo wären die zehn Stämme Israels zu suchen?* Dr. M. Lewin, Frankfort, 1901.

167  It should be remembered that *Cush* in ancient Jewish literature does not always signify Ethiopia, but also denotes parts of Arabia, especially those nearest to Abyssinia. The name *Cush* is also applied to countries east of the Tigris, see p. 63.

168  Rayy is the ancient city of Rages, spoken of in the Book of Tobit i. 14. The ruins are in the neighbourhood of Teheran.

169  The incidents here related are fully gone into by Dr. Neubauer in the third of his valuable articles "Where are the ten tribes?" (*J. Q. R.*, vol. I, p. 185). There can be little doubt that the Kofar-al-Turak, a people belonging to the Tartar stock, are identical with the so-called subjects of Prester John, of whom so much was heard in the Middle Ages. They defeated Sinjar in the year 1141; this was, however, more than fifteen years prior to Benjamin's visit. To judge from the above passage, where the allies of the Jews are described as "infidels, the sons of Ghuz of the Kofar-al-Turak," Benjamin seems to confound the Ghuzes with the Tartar hordes. Now the Ghuzes belonged to the Seldjuk clans who had become Mohammedans more than 100 years before, and, as such,

Benjamin would never have styled them infidels. These Ghuzes waged war with Sinjar in 1153, when he was signally defeated, and eventually made prisoner. It is to this battle that Benjamin must have made reference, when he writes that it took place fifteen years ago. See Dr. A. Müller's *Islam,* also Dr. G. Oppert's *Presbyter Johannes in Sage und Geschichte, 1864.*

170  It will be noted that Benjamin uses here the terms יורד אדם, הוזר אדם, evidently implying that he himself did not go to sea.

In the Middle Ages the island of Kish or Kis was an important station on the trade route from India to Europe. Le Strange writes, p. 257, that in the course of the twelfth century it became the trade centre of the Persian Gulf. A great walled city was built in the island, where water-tanks had been constructed, and on the neighbouring sea-banks was the famous pearl-fishery. Ships from India and Arabia crowded the port. Kish was afterwards supplanted by Ormuz and Bandar-Abbas; England held possession of the island from 1820 to 1879, and it has recently been visited officially by Lord Curzon. For a description of the island see *The Times,* Jan. 18, 1904.

171  Katifa or El-Katif lies on the Persian Gulf, on the East coast of Arabia, near Bahrein. Bochart is of opinion that this part of Arabia is the land of Havilah, where, according to Gen. ii. 11 and 12, there is gold, bdellium, and the onyx stone. Jewish authorities are divided in opinion as to whether בדלה is a jewel, or the fragrant gum exuded by a species of balsam-tree. Benjamin follows Saadia Gaon, who in his Arabic translation of the Bible renders it הלולי, the very word used by our author here for pearls. Masudi is one of the earliest Arabic writers who gives us a description of the pearl-fisheries in the Persian Gulf, and it very much accords with Benjamin's account. See Sprenger's translation of Masudi's *Meadows of Gold,* p. 344. At the present time more

than 5,000 boats are engaged in this industry along this coast, and it yields an annual income of £1,000,000. See P. M. Sykes, *Ten Thousand Miles in Persia*, 1902.

172 Khulam, now called Quilon, was a much frequented seaport in the early Middle Ages where Chinese shippers met the Arab traders. It afterwards declined in importance, being supplanted by Calicut, Goa, and eventually by Bombay. It was situated at the southern end of the coast of Malabar. Renaudot in a translation of *The Travels of Two Mohammedan Traders*, who wrote as far back as 851 and 915 respectively, has given us some account of this place; Ibn Batuta and Marco Polo give us interesting details. Ritter, in the fifth volume of his Geography, dilates on the cultivation of the pepper-plant, which is of indigenous growth. In Benjamin's time it was thought that white pepper was a distinct species, but Ritter explains that it was prepared from the black pepper, which, after lying from eight to ten days in running water, would admit of being stripped of its black outer covering. Ritter devotes a chapter to the fire-worship of the Guebers, who, as Parsees, form an important element at the present day in the population of the Bombay Presidency. Another chapter is devoted to the Jewish settlement to which Benjamin refers. See *Die jüdischen Colonien in Indien*, Dr. Gustav Oppert; also *Semitic Studies*, (Berlin,1897), pp. 396-419.

Under the heading of "Cochin", the Jewish Encyclopaedia gives an account of the White and Black Jews of Malabar. By way of supplementing the Article, it may be well to refer to a MS., No. 4238 of the Merzbacher Library formerly at Munich. It is a document drawn up in reply to eleven questions addressed by Tobias Boas on the 12 Ellul 5527 (= 1767) to R. Jeches Kel Rachbi of Malabar. From this MS. it appears that 10,000 exiled Jews reached Malabar A. C. 68 (i. e. about the time of the destruction of the Second Temple) and settled at Cranganor, Dschalor, Madri and Plota. An extract of this MS. is given in Winter and Wünsche's *Jüdische Literatur*, vol III, p. 459. Cf. article on the Beni-Israel of India by Samuel B. Samuel, *The Jewish Literary Annual*, 1905.

173 The British Museum text has Ibrig, and the Casanatense has Ibriag: neither can be identified. The printed editions have איי כנדג the islands of Candig, which Asher thinks may be taken to refer to Ceylon, having regard to the name of the capital, Kandy. It was not the capital in Benjamin's time. The difficulty still remains that it does not take twenty-three days, but about four days, to reach Ceylon from Quilon. Renaudot states that in the tenth century a multitude of Jews resided in the island, and that they took part in the municipal government as well as other sects, as the King granted the utmost religious liberty. See Pinkerton's *Travels*, vol. VII, p. 217. A full description is also given of the ceremonial when any notability proceeds to immolate himself by committing himself to the flames.

174 Benjamin's statements as to India and China are of course very vague, but we must remember he was the first European who as much as mentions China. Having regard to the full descriptions of other countries of the old World by Arabic writers of the Middle Ages, and to the fact that the trade route then was principally by sea on the route indicated by Benjamin, it is surprising that we have comparatively little information about India and China from Arabic sources. In none of their records is the Sea of Nikpa named, and it is not improbable that Benjamin coined this name himself from the root קפא which occurs in the Bible four times; in the Song of Moses (Exod. xv. 8): קפאו תהומות בלב ים "The depths were curdled in the heart of the sea" (not "*congealed*" as the Version has it), Job x. 10: כגבינה תקפיאני "curdled me like cheese"; and in Zeph. i. 12 and Zech. xiv. 6. The term "the curdling sea" would be very expressive of the tempestuous nature

of the China Sea and of some of its straits at certain seasons of the year.

175 Marco Polo has much to say about the bird "gryphon" when speaking of the sea-currents which drive ships from Malabar to Madagascar. He says, vol. II, book III, chap. 33: "It is for all the world like an eagle, but one indeed of enormous size. It is so strong that it will seize an elephant in its talons and carry him high into the air and drop him so that he is smashed to pieces; having so killed him, the gryphon swoops down on him and eats him at leisure. The people of those isles call the bird 'Rukh.'" Yule has an interesting note (vol. II, p. 348) showing how old and widespread the fable of the Rukh was, and is of opinion that the reason that the legend was localized in the direction of Madagascar was perhaps that some remains of the great fossil Aepyornis and its colossal eggs were found in that island. Professor Sayce states that the Rukh figures much—not only in Chinese folk-lore—but also in the old, Babylonian literature. The bird is of course familiar to readers of *The Arabian Nights*.

176 Neither Al-Gingaleh nor Chulan can be satisfactorily identified. Benjamin has already made it clear that to get from India to China takes sixty-three days, that is to say twenty-three days from Khulam to Ibrig, and thence forty days to the sea of Nikpa. The return journey, not merely to India but to Zebid, which Abulfeda and Alberuni call the principal port of Yemen, seems to take but thirty-four days. With regard to Aden, the port long in England's possession, and the so-called first outpost of the Indian Empire, it has already been explained (p. 50) that this part of Arabia as well as Abyssinia on the other side of the Red Sea were considered part of Middle India. Ibn Batuta says about Aden: "It is situated on the sea-shore and is a large city, but without either seed, water, or tree. They have reservoirs in which they collect the rain for drinking. Some rich merchants reside here, and vessels from India

occasionally arrive." A Jewish community has been there from time immemorial. The men until recent times used to go about all day in their Tephillin. Jacob Saphir devotes vol. II, chaps, i-x of his *Eben Saphir*, to a full account of the Jews of Aden.

177 We must take Benjamin's statements here to mean that the independent Jews who lived in the mountainous country in the rear of Aden crossed the Straits of Bab-el-Mandeb and made war against the inhabitants of the Plains of Abyssinia. J. Lelewel, in a series of letters addressed to E. Carmoly, entitled *Examen géographique des Voyages de Benjamin de Tudèle* (Bruxelles, 1852), takes great pains to locate the land of Hommatum ארץ המעטום, in lieu of which our text reads הכישור ארץ, the land of the Plains; but he quite fails in this and in many other attempts at identification. The Jews coming from Aden had to encounter the forces of the Christian sovereign of Abyssinia, and sought safety in the mountainous regions of that country. Here they were heard of later under the name of Falasha Jews. Cf. Marco Polo, vol. III, chap. xxxv. The reader is referred to Colonel Yule's valuable notes to this chapter. He quotes Bruce's *Abstract of Abyssinian Chronicles* with regard to a Jewish dynasty which superseded the royal line in the tenth century. See also Dr. Charles Singer's interesting communication in *J. Q. R.*, XVII, p. 142, and J. Halevy's *Travels in Abyssinia* (Miscellany of Hebrew Literature: 2nd Series, p. 175).

178 Assuan, according to Makrizi, was a most flourishing town prior to 1403, when more than 20,000 of its inhabitants perished. Seba cannot be identified. No doubt our author alludes to Seba, a name repeatedly coupled in Scripture with Egypt, Cush and Havilah.

179 Heluan is the present Helwan, fourteen miles from Cairo, which was greatly appreciated by the early Caliphs for its thermal sulphur springs. Stanley Lane Poole, in *The Story of Cairo*, p. 61, tells us of its edifices, and adds: "It is curious to consider how nearly this

modern health-resort became the capital of Egypt." Heluan is situated on the right bank of the Nile. One would have thought that the caravans proceeding to the interior of Africa through the Sahara Desert would have started from the left bank of the Nile; but we must remember that ancient Memphis, which stood on the left bank and faced Heluan, had been abandoned long before Benjamin's time. Edrisi and Abulfeda confirm Benjamin's statement respecting Zawila or Zaouyla, which was the capital of Gana—the modern Fezzan—a large oasis in the Sahara Desert, south of Tripoli.

180 This sentence is out of place, and should follow the sentence in the preceding paragraph which speaks of the Sultan Al-Habash.

181 Kutz, the present Kus, is halfway between Keneh and Luxor. The old town, now entirely vanished, was second in size to Fostat, and was the chief centre of the Arabian trade. The distance of Kus from Fayum is about 300 miles. The letter ש letter 'Sin' denotes 300, not 3.

182 In the Middle Ages the Fayum was wrongly called Pithom. E. Naville has identified the ruins of Tell-el-Maskhuta near Ismailieh with Pithom, the treasure city mentioned in Exodus i. 11. Among the buildings, grain-stores have been discovered in the form of deep rectangular chambers without doors, into which the corn was poured from above. These are supposed to date from the time of Rameses II. See *The Store City of Pithom and the Route of the Exodus*: A Memoir of the Egypt Exploration Fund. E. Naville, 1885. The Fayum, or Marsh-district, owes its extraordinary fertility to the Bahr Yussuf (Joseph's Canal).

The Arab story is that when Joseph was getting old the courtiers tried to bring about his disgrace by inducing Pharaoh to set him what appeared to be an impossible task, viz. to double the revenues of the province within a few years. Joseph accomplished the task by artificially adapting a natural branch of the Nile so as to give the district the benefit of the yearly overflow. The canal thus formed, which is 207 miles in length, was called after Joseph. The storehouses of Joseph are repeatedly mentioned by Arabic writers. Cf. Koran xii. 55, *Jacut*, IV, 933 and *Makrizi*, I, 241.

183 'Mr. Israel Abrahams, in *J. Q. R.*, XVII, 427 sqq., and Mr. E. J. Worman, vol. XVIII, 1, give us very interesting information respecting Fostat and Cairo, as derived from Geniza documents, but to comprehend fully Benjamin's account, we must remember that at the time of his visit the metropolis was passing through a crisis. Since March, 1169, Saladin had virtually become the ruler of Egypt, although nominally he acted as Vizier to the Caliph El-Adid, who was the last of the Fatimite line, and who died Sept. 13, 1171, three days after his deposition. The student is referred to the biography of Saladin by Mr. Stanley Lane Poole, 1878. Chap, viii gives a full account of Cairo as at 1170 and is accompanied by a map. The well-known citadel of Cairo, standing on the spurs of the Mukattam Hills, was erected by Saladin seven years later. The Cairo of 1170, which was styled El Medina, and was called by Benjamin ארמון צוען המדינה, was founded in 969, and consisted of an immense palace for the Caliph and his large household. It was surrounded by quarters for a large army, and edifices for the ministers and government offices. The whole was protected by massive walls and imposing Norman-like gates. The civil population—more particularly the Jews—dwelt in the old Kasr-esh-Shama quarter round the so-called Castle of Babylon, also in the city of Fostat, founded in 641, and in the El-Askar quarter, which was built in 751. These suburbs went under the name of Misr or Masr, but are called by Benjamin "Mizraim." Fostat was set on fire on Nov. 12, 1168, by the order of the Vizier Shawar, in order that it might not give shelter to the Franks who had invaded Egypt, but was soon rebuilt in part. It now goes

under the name Masr-el-Atika, and is noted at the present day for its immense rubbish heaps. See Stanley Lane Poole's *Cairo*, p. 34.

184 Cf. two elaborate papers by Dr. A. Büchler, "The Reading of the Law and Prophets in a Triennial Cycle," *J. Q. R.*, V, 420, VI, I, and E. N. Adler, ib. VIII, 529. For details as to synagogues, see *J. Q. R.*, XVIII, 11; Letter I of R. Obadja da Bertinoro; *Miscellany of Hebrew Literature*, p. 133; Joseph Sambari's Chronicle in Dr. Neubauer's *Anecdota Oxoniensia*, p. 118. Sambari must have had Benjamin's *Itinerary* before him, as has been pointed out by Mr. I. Abrahams, *J. Q. R.*, II, 107.

185 Zunz was the first to put forward the supposition that R. Nethanel is identical with Hibet Allah ibn al Jami, who later on became Saladin's physician (Asher, vol. II, p. 253). Graetz, vol. VI, p. 307, inclines to the same view. Dr. Steinschneider, *Die arabische Literatur der Juden*, 1902, p. 178, confirms this opinion, and gives a detailed account of Hibet Allah's medical and philosophical works. Dr. Neubauer, in an article, *J.Q.R.*, VIII, 541, draws attention to a Geniza fragment which contains a marriage contract dated 1160, wherein R. Nethanel is called a Levite. Benjamin does not style him so here. The same article contains the so-called Suttah Megillah, on which Professor Kaufmann comments, *J.Q.R.*, X, p. 171. It would appear that R. Nethanel never attained the dignity of Nagid. During Benjamin's visit to Egypt Sutta, in his capacity of Chief Collector of Taxes, filled nominally that office. Later on, after Sutta's fall, the dignity of Nagid was offered to Moses Maimonides, but was not accepted by him.

186 This term (which is not given in the printed editions) means that the people were followers of Ali, the son-in-law of Mohammed, founder of the Shiite sect.

187 This same Nilometer is readily shown to the visitor at the south end of the Island of Roda, which is accessible by means of a ferry-boat from the Kasr-esh Shama, not far from the Kenisat

Eliyahu, where the Geniza manuscripts were found. See E. N. Adler's *Jews in Many Lands*, p. 28, also *J.Q.R.*, IX, 669. The Nilometer is in a square well 16 feet in diameter, having in the centre a graduated octagonal column with Cufic inscriptions, and is 17 cubits in height, the cubit being 21-1/3 inches. The water of the Nile, when at its lowest, covers 7 cubits of the Nilometer, and when it reaches a height of 15-2/3 cubits the Sheikh of the Nile proclaims the Wefa, i.e., that the height of the water necessary for irrigating every part of the Nile valley has been attained. The signal is then given for the cutting of the embankment. We know that the column of the Nilometer has been frequently repaired, which fact explains the apparent discrepancy between the height of the gauge as given in Benjamin's narrative and the figures just mentioned.

188 It has only been established quite recently that the periodical inundations of the Nile are not caused by the increased outflow from the lakes in Central Africa, inasmuch as this outflow is quite lost in the marshy land south of Fashoda. Moreover, the river is absolutely blocked by the accumulation of the Papyrus weed, known as Sudd, the סוּף êis of Scripture, Exod. ii. 3-5. The inundations are brought about purely by the excessive rains in the highlands of Abyssinia, which cause the flooding of the Blue Nile and the Atbara in June and July and of the lower Nile in August and September.

189 In a Geniza fragment C quoted by Dr. Neubauer in *J.Q.R.*, IX, p. 36, this city is called אִישְׁמוֹשְׁטָמָאִיתִי . Probably the first two letters denote that it is an island. Compare the passage in Schechter's *Saadyana*, pp. 90, 91, וימלך על נא אמון ואי חנס ואי כפתור .

190 Ashmun is described by Abulfeda as a large city. We read in a Geniza fragment that David ben Daniel, a descendant of the

Exilarch, passed through this place on the way to Fostat, *J.Q.R.*, XV, 87. The fourth channel is the Tanitic branch. See p. 78, n. 2.

191 See Koran xii. 55. Sambari, who being a native of Egypt knew Cairo well, explains very fully, p. 119, that Masr-el-Atika is not here referred to, but ancient Memphis, the seat of royalty in Joseph's time. He explains that it was situated on the left side of the Nile, two parasangs distant from Cairo. See Reinaud's *Abulfeda*, vol. II, p. 140.

192 See *Makrizi*, vol. II, 464, and *J.Q.R.*, XV, p. 75; also XIX, 502.

193 E. Naville in his *Essay on the Land of Goshen*, being the fifth Memoir of the Egypt Exploration Fund, 1887, comes to the conclusion that the land of Goshen comprised the triangle formed by Bilbais, Zakazig, and Tel-el-Kebir. He is of opinion that the land of Ramses included the land of Goshen, and is that part of the Delta which lies to the eastward of the Tanitic branch of the Nile. The capital of the province—the Egyptian nome of Arabia—was the Phakusa of the Greeks. A small railway station is now on the spot, which bears the name Ramses. Cf. Gen. xlvii. 11.

194 Ain-al-Shams was situated three parasangs from Fostat, according to Jacut (III, 762), who records that in his day the place showed many traces of buildings from Pharaoh's time. Benha is now a somewhat important railway station about thirty miles north of Cairo. Muneh Sifte is a station on the Damietta arm of the Nile.

195 Samnu is perhaps Samnat, Dukmak, V, 20. On Damira see Schechter, *Saadyana*, p. 82; Worman, *J.Q.R.*, XVIII, 10. The zoologist Damiri was born here. Lammanah in the other versions is Mahallat or Mehallet-el-Kebir, mentioned by Abulfeda as a large city with many monuments, and is now a railway station between Tanta and Mansura. Sambari (119, 10) mentions a synagogue there, to which Jews even now make pilgrimages (Goldziher, *Z.D.P.G.*, vol. XXVIII, p. 153).

196 In the Middle Ages certain biblical names were without valid reason applied to noted places. No-Ammon mentioned in Scripture (Jer. xlvi. 25 and Nahum iii. 8), also in cuneiform inscriptions, was doubtless ancient Thebes. See Robinson, *Biblical Researches*, vol. I, p. 542. Another notable example is the application of the name of Zoan to Cairo. Ancient Tanis (p. 78) was probably Zoan, and we are told (Num. xiii. 22) that Zoan was built seven years after Hebron. It can be traced as far back as the sixth dynasty—over 2,000 years before Cairo was founded.

197 Josephus, who had the opportunity of seeing the Pharos before it was destroyed, must likewise have exaggerated when he said that the lighthouse threw its rays a distance of 300 stadia. Strabo describes the Pharos of Alexandria, which was considered one of the wonders of the world. As the coast was low and there were no landmarks, it proved of great service to the city. It was built of white marble, and on the top there blazed a huge beacon of logs saturated with pitch. Abulfeda alludes to the large mirror which enabled the lighthouse keepers to detect from a great distance the approach of the enemy. He further mentions that the trick by which the mirror was destroyed took place in the first century of Islamism, under the Caliph Valyd, the son of Abd-almalek.

198 It will be seen that the list of names given in our text is much more complete than that given by Asher, who enumerates but twenty-eight Christian states in lieu of forty given in the British Museum MS. In some cases the readings of R and O, which appear to have been written by careful scribes, and are of an older date than E and the printed editions, have been adopted. In our text, through the ignorance of the scribe, who had no gazetteer or map to turn to, some palpable errors have crept in. For instance, in naming Amalfi, already mentioned on p. 9, the error in spelling it מכיל has been repeated. Patzinakia (referred to on p. 12, as trading with Constantinople) is there spelt

ורוּשׂוּ .בִּיצִינִי not פִּיסִינָה may be read וִיחסֹר; ; I have rendered it Hainault in accordance with Deguigne's *Memoir*, referred to by Asher. Maurienne (mentioned p. 79) embraced Savoy and the Maritime Alps. It was named after the Moors who settled there.

199   Simasin or Timasin is doubtless near Lake Timsah. Sunbat is spoken of by Arabic writers as noted for its linen manufactures and trade.

200   Elim has been identified with Wadi Gharandel. It is reached in two hours from the bitter spring in the Wadi Hawara, believed to be the *Marah* of the Bible. Burckhardt conjectures that the juice of the berry of the gharkad, a shrub growing in the neighbourhood, may have the property, like the juice of the pomegranate, of improving brackish water; see p. 475, Baedecker's *Egypt*, 1879 edition. Professor Lepsius was responsible for the chapter on the Sinai routes.

201   A journey of two days would bring the traveller to the luxuriant oasis of Firan, which ancient tradition and modern explorers agree in identifying as Rephidim. From Firan it is held, by Professor Sayce and others, that the main body of the Israelites with their flocks and herds probably passed the Wadi esh-Shekh, while Moses and the elders went by Wadi Selaf and Nakb el-Hawa. The final camping-ground, at which took place the giving of the Law, is supposed to be the Raha plain at the foot of the peak of Jebel Musa. It may be mentioned that some explorers are of opinion that Mount Serbal was the mountain of revelation. There are authorities who maintain that Horeb was the name of the whole mountain range, Sinai being the individual mountain; others think that Horeb designated the northern range and Sinai the southern range. See Dr. Robinson's *Biblical Researches*, vol. I, section iii: also articles *Sinai* in Cheyne's *Encyclopaedia Biblica* and Dean Stanley's *Sinai and Palestine*.

202    The monastery of St. Catherine was erected 2,000 feet below the summit of Jebel Musa. It was founded by Justinian to give shelter to the numerous Syrian hermits who inhabited the peninsula. The monastery was presided over by an Archbishop.

203    The passage in square brackets is inserted from the Oxford MS. The city of Tur, which Benjamin calls Tur-Sinai, is situated on the eastern side of the Gulf of Suez, and affords good anchorage, the harbour being protected by coral reefs. It can be reached from the monastery in little more than a day. The small mountain referred to by Benjamin is the Jebel Hammam Sidna Musa, the mountain of the bath of our lord Moses.

204    Tanis, now called San, was probably the Zoan of Scripture, but in the Middle Ages it was held to be Hanes, mentioned in Isa. xxx. 4. It was situated on the eastern bank of the Tanitic branch of the Nile, about thirty miles south-west of the ancient Pelusium. The excavations which have been made by M. Mariette and Mr. Flinders Petrie prove that it was one of the largest and most important cities of the Delta. It forms the subject of the Second Memoir of the Egypt Exploration Fund, 1885. The place must not be confounded with the seaport town Tennis, as has been done by Asher. In the sixth century the waters of the Lake Menzaleh invaded a large portion of the fertile Tanis territory. Hence Benjamin calls it an island in the midst of the sea. In a Geniza document dated 1106, quoted by Dr. Schechter, *Saadyana*, p. 91, occurs the passage:

" במדינת אי חנס דביניך ימה מותבה ולשון נחל מצרים הקרוי נילוס

In the city of the isle Hanes, which is in the midst of the sea and of the tongue of the river of Egypt called Nile."

205    The straits of Messina were named Faro. Lipar has reference, no doubt, to the Liparian Islands, which are in the neighbourhood.

206 Cf. Bertinoro's interesting description of the synagogue at Palermo, which he said had not its equal, *Miscellany of Hebrew Literature*, vol. I, p. 114.

207 Hacina is the Arabic for a fortified or enclosed place.

208 Buheira is the Arabic word for a lake. The unrivalled hunting grounds of William II are well worth visiting, being situated between the little town called Parco and the magnificent cathedral of Monreale, which the king erected later on.

209 King William II, surnamed "the Good," was sixteen years old when Benjamin visited Sicily in 1170. During the king's minority the Archbishop was the vice-regent. He was expelled in 1169 on account of his unpopularity. Asher asserts that Benjamin's visit must have taken place prior to this date, because he reads כי היא מדינת סגן המלך *This is the domain of the viceroy*. The Oxford MS. agrees with our text and reads כי היא מדינת גן המלך *This is the domain of the king's garden*. Chroniclers tell that when the young king was freed from the control of the viceroy he gave himself up to pleasure and dissipation. Asher is clearly wrong, because a mere boy could not have indulged in those frolics. The point is of importance, as it absolutely fixes the date of Benjamin's visit to the island. It was in the year 1177 that William married the daughter of our English king, Henry II.

210 Edrisi, who wrote his Geography in Sicily in 1154 at the request of King Roger II, calls the island a pearl, and cannot find words sufficient in praise of its climate, beauty, and fertility. He is especially enthusiastic concerning Palermo. Petralia is described by him as being a fortified place, and an excellent place of refuge, the surrounding country being under a high state of cultivation and very productive. Asher has no justification for reading Pantaleoni instead of Petralia.

211 The passage in square brackets is to be found in most of the printed editions, as well as in the Epstein (E) MS., which is so

much akin to them, and is comparatively modern. The style will at once show that the passage is a late interpolation, and the genuine MSS. now forthcoming omit it altogether.

212 See Aronius, *Regester*, p. 131. This writer, as a matter of course, had only the printed editions before him. His supposition that משתראן is Mayence is more than doubtful, but his and Lelewel's identification of מרנמרק with Mantern and נמייש with Freising has been accepted. Aronius casts doubts as to whether Benjamin actually visited Germany, in the face of his loose statements as to its rivers. It will now be seen that he is remarkably correct in this respect.

213 The Jews of Prague are often spoken of in contemporary records. Rabbi Pethachia started on his travels from Ratisbon, passing through Prague on his way to Poland and Kieff.

214 Benjamin does not tell us whether Jews resided in Kieff. Mr. A. Epstein has obligingly furnished the following references: In ואמוראים סדר הנאים, Graetz, *Monatsschrift*, 39, 511, we read: ראש ישיבות וה״ר ר׳ משה מקיוב שאל את פי. In סדר הישר, *Monatsschrift*, 40, 134, כמו ר משה מקיוב מפי רבינו תם. This Rabbi Moses is also mentioned in *Resp.* of R. Meir of Rothenburg, ed. Berlin, p. 64. Later records give the name ר׳ משה בר יעקב הגולה מקיוב.

215 The vair (vaiverge or wieworka in Polish) is a species of marten, often referred to in mediaeval works. Menu-vair is the well-known fur miniver.

216 Lelewel, having the reading אל סודו before him, thought Sedan was here designated. H. Gross suspected that the city of Auxerre, situated on the borders of the province of the Isle de France, the old patrimony of the French kings, must have been intended, and the reading of our text proves him to be right. The Roman name Antiossiodorum became converted into Alciodorum, then Alcore, and finally into Auxerre. The place is often cited in our mediaeval literature, as it was a noted seat of learning. The great

men of Auxerre, גדולי אלשורא, joined the Synod convened by Rashbam and Rabenu Tam. See *Gallia Judaica*, p. 60, also Graetz, vol. VI, 395 (10).

# BIBLIOBAZAAR

## The essential book market!

Did you know that you can get any of our titles in large print?

Did you know that we have an ever-growing collection of books in many languages?

**Order online:**
**www.bibliobazaar.com**

Find all of your favorite classic books!

Stay up to date with the latest government reports!

At BiblioBazaar, we aim to make knowledge more accessible by making thousands of titles available to you- *quickly and affordably*.

Contact us:
BiblioBazaar
PO Box 21206
Charleston, SC 29413

LaVergne, TN USA
26 January 2010
171227LV00006B/62/A